Pieces

From the attic of my mind

Tom Cooney

Skytop Books

Brookville, Indiana

Pieces

From the attic of my mind

First Edition

ISBN 13:978-1717239396

Author's Note

I was born into an exclusive yet extensive club, the post WW2 babies known as the Boomers. Democracy had prevailed, evil had been crushed, the perfect time for making love. And so, they did, our parents, with great enthusiasm, hope and expectation, they went forth and multiplied.

I have now entered another exclusive club. I am a geezer. You can call me an old fart if you like. Just don't call me a senior, a cab or late for dinner. Clinically I might be called chronologically challenged, facing far more shadows than horizons. I am trying hard to earn the rank of curmudgeon, embracing the stereotypes associated which ageing and pushing the limits to see how much I can get away with. I never thought I'd live so long. Now that I have, I feel I have the right to assert myself. Who knows where this might lead me, face down with a bloody nose in a gutter, or revered as a wise old man. Time will tell.

I was motivated to write this book by the feeling that I should practice what I preach before my time runs out. For years now, I have been urging others to write about their lives, believing in the cathartic power of reflection and the need for future generations to know who we were, seeking more than names and dates, but actual voices from the past. Every story deserves to be told. You are important enough. Don't let modesty or lack of finely developed writing skills get in the way. If you don't like writing, sit down and record your spoken word. Perhaps a child or grandchild might enjoy interviewing you.

`Autobiographies are for the masses, not just the rich, famous and infamous. But this book is definitely not a true autobiography. It is a collection of stories inspired by flashbacks I get from time to time, vivid images of moments and events that spring forth, often without any obvious provocation.

I started writing a long time ago, back before the internet. Following the advice of teachers to "write about what you know," I wrote memories of my life growing up with six siblings in a row house in Philadelphia. These pieces were very popular with family members, though many were quick to point out what they thought I had gotten wrong. From this I leaned that reality is elusive. Shared experiences come with various interpretations of what actually happened, and what it all meant. No wonder folks have such different views related to politics and world events.

But I was determined to not let disputed facts get in the way of a good story. These are my memories, from my attic, and I call them like I see them.

In 1979, I moved with my wife and nine-month-old son to rural Franklin County, Indiana, where my wife was born and raised. I began writing humorous pieces about my transition from city boy to country boy. These too, were well received by both my family and friends back in Philly and my new friends and acquaintances in the little town I grew to love. The arrival of the internet and Facebook encouraged me to write more.

This book is mostly a collection of pieces I have written over the years. I have posted many of them on Facebook. For this book, many of these have been expanded, modified, corrected, and manipulated to such an extent that, if you do follow me on Facebook, you may actually find these pieces to be fresh and new. My vision of the past keeps changing over time. I like to think of it as improving, as I wander back, revisit and reconsider things.

I have also included some works of fiction, and some works of whimsy, never before revealed, perhaps for good reason. You be the judge. I do hope you enjoy the book. The pieces are short. You can pick it up and start anywhere, flip back and forth to whatever piece catches your fancy. It is an easy read. It may not change your life in any way, but I would be most pleased if it provides you with some amusement, and the determination to tell your own stories.

Tom Cooney

"The past is an old armchair in the attic, the present an ominous ticking sound, and the future is anybody's guess."

James Thurber

Introduction

While rummaging around in my attic recently, I made a strange discovery. In a dark corner I saw a pile of stuff that apparently had not been touched for many years. I was drawn to it and began going through the pile piece by piece, peeling off layer after layer of long forgotten things. Many brought memories and seemed worth keeping but I tend to keep stuff much too long, after any value, personal, practical or commercial, has diminished and faded.

Several layers down I found an old jigsaw puzzle box, aged and worn and falling apart. One corner was torn open completely and several pieces had fallen out and were scattered on the floor. I picked up the box to get a closer view of the image on the lid, scattering more pieces in the process.

To my complete shock, I saw my own image on the top, in profile, from the shoulders up. It was a photo of me as I am today, but with a most bizarre twist. In the front of my head the flesh was gone, exposing part of my brain. Behind my ear was a ladder leaning up inside my head. It was in vibrant color. How could this be? What did it mean?

I fell to my knees. It took me several minutes to recover enough to come to grips with what I held in my hands. There was no explanation I could think of. How could a distorted picture of me as I am today possibly be on the cover of this old puzzle box? I picked out a piece and looked at it carefully. It was definitely a clean, new fraction of an image somehow printed on very old cardboard.

Hastily, I gathered up all the pieces I could see scattered around and placed them back in the box. I stood up and carefully carried the box down the ladder from the attic to my den.

There I was able to view the box much better. There was nothing else on it but the strange photo, no words at all, no indication of where it came from or how many pieces it contained.

I was alone in the house. My wife was off visiting her aunt in California and would not be back for several days. I set up a card table and began sorting the pieces, looking for the edge pieces as I usually do with jigsaw puzzles. Completing the perimeter would determine the size. Just as I made the first connection of two edge pieces I got another shock, a physical one this time. It started as a slight tingling sensation in my fingers, like a mild jolt of electricity, but quickly sped up to my head where it intensified. It was as if I could feel the signals passing from one nerve cell to another in my brain setting off synaptic fireworks. I then quickly drifted back in time, feeling, smelling, reliving an episode from my childhood. Instinctively, I lifted my fingers and the sensation abruptly stopped. I was back to the here and now.

Tentatively, I connected two more pieces and it happened again, taking me to a different period of my life. This was not just reminiscence. It was total immersion, like diving into a pool, breaking the surface of the water separating two worlds, swimming deeper and deeper and then slowly rising to the surface, back to the here and now. It was frightening but exhilarating. I wanted to do it again and again.

Each connection, each dive, brought forth another episode, starting with my world before I was born and moving along as I grew up. I know this sounds very strange and unbelievable. It certainly was to me. I have no way of explaining it.

The following stories are an attempt to document these experiences of my past as best I can, realizing that my words cannot fully capture what they were like for me.

Before my time

Helen held the flashlight, trying not to tremble, as her mother typed. She had volunteered Mom to type for the nuns at her elementary school. Mom was one of the only mothers in the neighborhood who had graduated from high school and learned to type, or perhaps the only one who admitted to learning the skill.

This was during the Second World War and there were nightly air raid drills. All lights in her Philadelphia neighborhood, like many neighborhoods and rural homes across the continent, had to be turned off. Air raid wardens roamed the streets to enforce the lights-out policy. But the nuns needed the typing to be done.

Helen was fearful they would be caught by the warden. But she was more frightened that a Japanese plane would see the light and drop a bomb on the house. The house would be destroyed and all the family as well. And it would be Helen's fault since she volunteered Mom to type for the nuns.

Fortunately, that bomb never dropped. If it had I would never have been born. I have heard this story and so many other family stories repeated over and over again throughout my life. Over the years I have gotten better at asking questions and picking up new details about family life before me. They seem a part of me now.

I feel like I was there when we stood outside on the grass and waved at the children several stories up in the Shriners Hospital where sister Ann spent way too much of her childhood going through orthopedic surgeries on her bad hip. Children were not allowed to visit the wards. I can feel the summer air and see all the children waving from above. I can hear their voices. Yet, when I do the math, I realize that if I had been there at all I would have been a babe in arms at best, unable to remember the experience. Such false memories are so rich in detail that they are indistinguishable at times from the events I do remember.

Certainly, I was not there when Mom and Dad met at a Saint Patrick's Day party. Certainly, I was not there sometime later when they were engaged. But I can see it all as Dad told it. He was driving Mom across the Betsy Ross Bridge in his Model A Ford when they were stuck in traffic. Mom hopped out of the car, climbed the rail and threatened to jump unless Dad married her. I can see it all, although the story was always fiercely disputed by Mom and never actually happened.

I was not yet born when Helen held the flashlight while Mom typed, but I can feel her fear, waiting for the bomb to fall. I would have not been a direct causality of the blast, but a yet-to-be-born one.

The Vote

'Twas during the heady years after World War II that this tale takes place. Democracy was king and justice prevailed in half-hour segments through the righteous power of cowboy heroes on the TV set. But our house was in turmoil. Furniture was turned over and Danny and Chucky, my older brothers, were leaping about and generally challenging the authority of Helen, the oldest sib and appointed surrogate mother. Baby sister, Kathy, was crying and desperately in need of a diaper change. I was barely out of diapers myself, my grasp of situations rather limited. But I could hear and see and feel the sense of chaos.

Chucky's favorite cowboy was Hop-along Cassidy, Danny's was Gene Autry and mine was Roy Rogers. It was way past my bed time. Mom was at her new job, working in the cafeteria of a factory. She had to take the trolley and a bus to get there and we were not supposed to try to reach her by phone. If there was a problem, we were instructed to walk up the street to Carolyn's, the Irish Bar where dad worked his second job as bartender. This was only to be done in case of an emergency.

Words flew like bullets from a six-shooter, held at the hip and rapidly fired. Some issue of fairness became the target. I had no idea what the discussion was about. It came down to two choices and my brothers forced a vote. Helen, Ann and Charlotte voted one way, and my two brothers the other. Suddenly they all looked at me. Ann got the baby to stop crying. All was suddenly silent.

My birth had been eagerly anticipated by my siblings for just such moments. If I had been a girl, my sisters would have the edge. Baby Kathy was too little to vote yet. I was totally befuddled by the issues at hand, but I decided quickly. I cast my lot with the boys. They didn't often treat me kindly, and I could not understand how they could like Gene and Hop-along better than Roy, but the good cowboys had to stick together.

A tied vote meant we would all have to put on our hats and coats and walk up the block to the bar.

Fifth Street was alive with trolley cars, autos and lamp posts lighting up the dark. Ann carried Kathy. This one side of one block of row houses in Philadelphia was my world, yet it was transformed by night almost beyond recognition. I was distracted by how familiar yet different it all was, injected with a new, raw energy. The shops were dark inside, but most of the windows pulsated with the cold light of neon. I had trouble keeping up.

We reached the bar and paused to look down the narrow, dark alley between it and the neighboring store. The tall brick walls were broken only by a door near the alley's end and the small lighted sign above it with the word "Ladies". This is where we had to go. We walked in single file with Helen and Chucky in the lead. We lined up by the door and Helen knocked. We could hear the muffled sounds of gayety inside, but no one answered. My brothers pounded harder, again and again, until the door finally opened.

Laughter, light, and strange aromas burst into the alley. I was nearly blown over by the sudden assault on my senses. A woman stood before us, back lit by the boisterous scene inside and wobbling slightly from side to side. Before she could speak we told her that we had to talk to our daddy who was the bartender, all urgently pleading at once. She turned and yelled "Charlie!" and we heard the name repeated by other unseen faces as the door swung back and closed on its spring. The roar of laughter grew behind the door.

It seemed like we waited forever, with a sense of dread and apprehension descending on us. Finally, the door flung open again, and there was dad. His figure filled the doorway. He stood with his arms akimbo, dressed in his long white apron, silhouetted by the bright lights and mayhem within, and looking like an all-powerful god. He was not happy to see us.

My brothers and sisters all started talking at once, explaining what happened, each with a melodramatic rendition of suffering and persecution. Dad quickly put a stop to that with a firm command. He wanted to hear us one at a time, starting with the eldest and going right down through the ranks. I listened intently as Helen began, but still could not get the slightest inkling of what this was all about. I said a little prayer, like mom taught me, praying that this would be resolved before he got to me. I would have no idea what to say. I was never so grateful to be so far down in the pecking order.

I was spared the humiliation. Somewhere along the line Dad had heard enough. He barked some precise and complicated orders that everyone except Kathy and me seemed to understand. We went back home and did what he said. No one was happy, but at least all was quiet. There was to be no bickering. That much I knew. I was soon put to bed. I thought of what I would have said if I had gotten a turn; probably something about Roy Rogers and how he always managed to get the bad guys and restore order when things seemed so hopeless. It was so amazing and comforting to know that there were guys like him and my dad in charge of the world.

I knew nothing of Nazis and fascists and the true evil that existed in the world. I knew nothing about the really bad things that can happen to good people. There was God and mom and dad, my sisters and brothers and Roy Rogers, and that was all I really needed. That was all I needed.

Epiphany

We lived on 5th Street in the Olney section of Philadelphia when I was little, moving to the Oxford Circle area when I was in the third grade. It was during my 5th Street years that I became aware of connections in my life as the circuitry of my brain developed. One day in particular stands out in this regard. I was standing on the sidewalk on Ashdale Street, our playground, more frequented by children than cars. I was watching the bigger kids. Two boys were throwing a ball back and forth. Smaller children ran back and forth between them. The two boys tried to catch the ball and tag the kids out before they got to a chalk-line base. That was called "runnin' bases". Up to then my life was a jumble of sights, sounds, activities, and sensations seemingly unrelated and unpredictable. Now I was starting to understand.

Ashdale Street was alive with the smell and feel of summer in the city. There was my brother, Chucky, throwing the ball so fast and far and gracefully, then catching the return throw and applying the tag so effortlessly. He was old, older than the kids who were running back and forth and trying to avoid the tags. They told me I was too little to play. I was barely out of diapers. But I could watch. I did and I learned.

My brother Danny was older too, but not as old as Chucky. They went to school in the big building across the street I was too little to cross on my own, behind the big church. They called it Inky Stinky and snickered. Mom didn't like them saying that. She called it Incarnation, and told me I would go there too when I was bigger. Sometimes I would stand on the corner and watch when they got out at the end of the school day. The bells would ring and the kids would pour out in single file in all directions, girls in their uniforms and boys in their white shirts, dark pants and school ties. The nuns would walk beside them with their clickers. They looked so strange and scary in their long black dresses and hoods, but mom said they were holy and good and married to God. Mom and Dad were married to each other.

My three big sisters were really old, even older than Chucky and Danny. Charlotte went to Inky too, but Ann and Helen got on the trolley and went to Little Flower. That's where the girls went when they got really big. My sisters talked a lot and played records, and talked a lot and twirled the baton so fast in the livin' room it made me scared. My brothers would yell at them and say they were gonna kill somebody. Helen was in charge when Mom and Dad were away, but my brothers wouldn't listen and would argue with the girls.

12

Girls and boys were different and didn't get along. I was a boy so I was supposed to agree with my brothers, but I usually didn't know what they were arguing about.

Oh yeah, I had a little sister too, but she was too little to count when it came to arguing. Her name was Kathy. She was so little she could hardly do anything yet. My big sisters liked to dress her up and play with her like she was a doll. She was a big star in the baby parade on the For-Fidg-July. The For-Fidg-July was almost as good as Christmas because there was lots of free ice cream and soda, caps and fire crackers, and a parade with flags and streamers and bikes with colored paper all over. Old men in funny uniforms would say the "pledge allegiance to the republic for Richard Stands". I didn't understand it, but it sounded really important. Then, when it got really dark, we'd all go to the high school, sit on blankets on the grass and watch the fireworks punch holes in the night.

It all was connected and it all was starting to make sense. We were lucky because we were Catholics and God liked us best. God was older than everybody in the world and could do anything and was invisible. We prayed to Him before we went to bed and when we went to His church. Praying was like talking to Him but I couldn't see Him or hear His voice.

As I stood there watching I felt that I was a part of all this, even though I was too little to play the game. Suddenly the ball sailed way over Chucky's head. He turned and chased it down the street as the kids dashed gleefully from base to base. I could see that it was headed for the sewer. If it went down there the game would stop. The big kids would have to get the top off of the sewer. Then they could get the ball with a rake, or lower a kid down head first to pluck the ball from the smelly water. Then they would have to wash it before they could use it again. But Chucky was a fast runner. He got there and caught the ball just before it got in the sewer. This was how it should be. This is how it was. We would always be family, even if we argued and didn't like each other at times. We would always be there to catch the ball, dress the baby, and watch the parade, or so it seemed.

Gospel

Long before I learn the catechism, I began to realize that there were certain truths that guided our lives. Some were difficult to understand. Some were painful. I learned that I would grow and be big like Daddy. But no matter how big I got, five of my six brothers and sisters would always be older than I am and, as far as I could tell, bigger and stronger. It just did not seem fair. We were constantly told to take turns. Why couldn't I get a turn at being the biggest?

Some truths helped regulate our lives, like the rhythmic movements of the sun and moon. Every day but Sunday the mailman would come. Sometimes, if it was warm and the windows were open, we could hear him come up the street. Then envelopes would push open the little slot next to the door and drop onto our living room floor. This was fascinating to me. Who was this man with the hand that so regularly invaded the sanctity of our home? I began to watch for him and study his dress, manner and movements. I played with the little slot until I learned that poking my fingers through from the inside could get my fingers stuck. I often watched my dad go off to work in the morning but had no idea what he did all day. The mailman I could study and copy. One day I took our letters and went up the street sticking one in each door. When mom found out she looked shocked. She went up the street to each house to retrieve the letters. Why was she undoing all my work?

When dad and my brothers and sisters got home and heard about this, everyone laughed. I tolerated them laughing at me without fuss. I thought they might all get mad at me the way my mom did at first. Mom said most of what we got in the mail was bills, and I should never again give them to the neighbors. What were bills, and why were they so important and private? They just seemed to make mom upset when they came. Who needed the darn things?

Sometimes, like a comet, the bill collector would come to the door. Often, when Mom could see him coming, she would tell us to close the blinds, turn out the lights and hide. Other times we had too little warning and she told us to tell him she was not home. At first, this was great fun, but over time the game wore thin. I didn't like seeing mom so upset, and couldn't see what the problem was. If Mr. Gresell was coming to collect bills, why didn't we give him all of ours? We had plenty, and we'd be sure to get more from the mailmen the next day. Mom didn't want them anyway.

Eventually I came to understand about the bills and why I should not deliver our mail to neighbors. But it seemed that, with each thing I was able to understand, another mystery would take its place.

The magic box

Before I started school, I spend my days with Mom and baby sister, Kathy, playing, fantasizing and looking out on my world. The busy street outside our door was very entertaining. I was mesmerized by vehicular traffic. I liked watching the trolley cars as they clanged along dropping off and picking up passengers at the corners. I watched the trucks intently, particularly when they stopped to pick up trash or make deliveries to homes and businesses. I especially liked it when they came to our house.

The milk truck was a regular visitor. The man in a crisp, white uniform would spring out and carry a container of glass milk bottles, set them at our door, pick up the empty bottles Mom left out, hop back in his truck and take off. Less frequently the coal truck would come, and men would slide a long metal chute from the back and stick the end in into our basement window. I got to watch as the black chunks of rock rattled down the chute, into the coal bin next to our furnace. This was all so interesting. It was hard to imagine anything more entertaining. Then one day that all changed.

A truck I had never seen before pulled up right in front of our house. Two men in brown uniforms got out. One opened the back of the truck and pulled out a ramp while the other came and knocked on our door. Mom spoke with him. I thought she was going to tell him they had the wrong house and send him away. But she didn't. The two men got into the back of the truck and slowly wheeled out a big cardboard box on an appliance dolly.

They carefully wheeled it down the ramp and into our house, setting it down in the middle of the living room floor. They cut around the bottom of the box and lifted it off. Mom signed some papers and away they went. There sat our new, very own television. It was a wooden cabinet much bigger than I was, and it had a big, twelve-inch screen. I wanted to turn it on but Mom said it was much too complicated, and that we needed to wait till Dad got home.

I knew what a TV was. Just about every day, late in the afternoon, my brothers and sister would walk me up the block and across the street. We would stand in front of the appliance store on the corner and stare at the TV in the window. We couldn't hear the sound, but we were mesmerized by the images. How could they possibly get all that inside that piece of furniture? I still sometimes marvel at that. We would stand there until my Dad, coming home from work, got off the trolley and we would walk him back home.

One day the owner of the store turned the set off while we were watching. The magic carpet was suddenly pulled out from under us and we were jolted back to life on the street. When we told Dad about this, he spoke with the store owner and, shortly after, decided he was going to buy one. Many years later I found out he took out a mortgage on the house to get it. Now here it was in our living room.

When Dad got home he made a space for the TV along a wall, hooked up the rabbit ears antenna, plugged it in and turned it on. No images appeared, just white haze. The only sound was a static buzz. But then Dad adjusted the fine-tuning dial and manipulated the rabbit ears until, sure enough, there were images of living people moving around, just like in the appliance store window. But we could hear them talking, and they were right in our living room.

So began our endless journey into worlds beyond our imagination. At first, we had no idea what would be on the screen and sometimes there would be nothing but a test pattern. During the first week we had the TV I discovered 'Willie the Worm' and 'Kukla, Fran and Ollie.' I was hooked. As time went on, more and more shows came into our home and I spent more and more of my time in front of the tube. I was on a slippery slope, a slide that would last most of my childhood, interfering with my school work and instilling a yearning to escape the crowded life of the city.

Kindergarten dropout

The nuns were at our door. My mother pleaded with me. But it was all over. I wasn't going back. I had almost made it through the first week of kindergarten when it happened. It came out of the blue. I was playing in the indoor sandbox next to Eddie. I didn't see him do anything bad, but he surely must have. The nun swooped down like lightening, grabbing him by the ear and bringing him to his feet. She was pinching his earlobe hard, almost lifting him off the floor by the ear. I had never seen anything like it.

She got our attention and told us she was going to show us what happens when we misbehave. She pulled Eddie by his ear over to a door and opened it. Inside there was a steep staircase leading down into a strange underground space. She called down for someone named Mr. Olson. He came up from the empty doom (AKA boiler room). He was a tall man in a dingy uniform. He grabbed Eddie by the arm and took him down into the hissing underworld.

The next day when I went to the school Eddie was not there. Was he still down in that nether world? Had he been eaten by that strange creature named Mr. Olsen? Somehow, I made it through that morning, but I was not going back, no way, no how, not ever.

Kindergarten was not mandatory, so my mother finally gave up trying to talk me into going back. For some reason, I never told her or anyone about what had happened. I guess I was so scared that, if I told anyone, that creature would come and get me.

This experience set the tone for the rest of my formal education, none of which I liked much at all, until I got to graduate school. But I got through the rest of it without being lifted up by the ear and eaten by a monster.

Boob Tube

Much of my early education came from television. Timmy lived on a farm and had a dog named Lassie. He had so much space to roam and play. Fields and woods, and the farm itself provided endless adventure. And if he got in any danger, like falling down a well or getting trapped in an abandoned mine shaft, Lassie was there to run and get help so he would be rescued. He was an only child and had his own bedroom and the full attention of his parents. He had a friend from a neighboring farm who joined him on adventures. I so envied him. I wanted to live in the country.

Then there was Roy Rogers, king of the cowboys, riding the range and rounding up bad guys, way out west, far from the city lights. Then came Superman, the strange visitor from another planet who became my hero and the focus of my rich fantasy life.

Then some years later came Spin and Marty. I got to see them the days they were on the 'Mickey Mouse Club.' Spin was a boy who lived with his uncle on a dude ranch. That was so cool. Marty was the rich, snob, city boy who arrived there for a summer camp, in his chauffeur driven limousine. Over the first season of the show they eventually got to be friends. I like seeing the city boy learn to be a country boy.

Then, in the second season of the show, the second season of the camp, their adventures took on a whole new dimension. The boy's camp hooked up with a girl's camp nearby, and there was Annette Funicello. This happened at a sensitive time for me, as I was just on the verge of being attracted to girls, rather than seeing them as a nuisance. Annette was also a Mouseketeer, and the only one with boobs.

It wasn't like I was totally unaware of boobs. I just sort of took them for granted and never thought about them much until Annette had them on TV. It wasn't like I could actually see them. She kept them well covered up, but they were definitely there, poking out through her sweater and bouncing around when she rode a horse with Spin and Marty. And those two boys certainly seemed to notice. They chased after her and fought over her. I wasn't sure why, but I thought it had something to do with her boobs.

So, I started looking around, and sure enough, they weren't just on TV. Lots of the girls in my neighborhood seemed to have them, even some who were very close to my age. Apparently, city girls had them too. Some seemed to sprout them overnight. What were they all about? I didn't understand them. So, I consulted my favorite reference book: the Sears catalogue. I had to do this on the sly, but I didn't know why. Instinctively I knew that what I was doing was sinful. I should not even think about what was going on under the clothing of girls. Yet I didn't seem to be able to stop myself.

The Sears catalogue was my bible for the world of commerce and culture. If I couldn't find it there it wasn't important. I was not disappointed. The book of Women's Wear had actual pictures of women in their underwear. I learned about bras and panties and the alluring category of lingerie. I was overwhelmed. I had to stop. I had too much. I had to sleep on all this. And sleep I did. But it wasn't visions of sugarplums that danced in my head, at least not literally.

S-E-X

We were forbidden to even say the word. It was a topic that was best not discussed, especially in front of the children. Saying the word was a sin, like saying a curse word. I was never told about the birds and bees by an adult. I was left on my own to figure it out, relying on my own observations and the dubious reports of other kids.

Mom was alone in the kitchen washing dishes when I popped a question, "Why don't nuns have babies?"

Her body suddenly froze. The suds dripped off the plate in her hand. Time seemed to slow down. Then, without looking at me, she said, "That's because they pray a lot."

Her body went back in motion, attacking the dirty dishes with determination and precision. That was it. I felt I had asked enough, but I was left confused. Mom prayed a lot and had seven babies. Maybe she prayed in the other direction, for kids rather than against them. If this was a piece of the puzzle it was a perplexing one.

Joey Corbin was a hyper-active kid in my third-grade class. He was lively and friendly, but once he was attracted to someone it was a bit like dealing with a persistent gnat. When I first encountered him in the school yard he wanted to know everything I knew about S-E-X, which was just about nothing, and I was not about to share with him my various lines of investigations. He knew far more than I did, and quickly became one of my resources.

Joey knew several curse words and was able to enlighten me about how several of them were connected to S-E-X. He suggested what the number 69 meant in this context. Many of the things he said were just too gross to believe. He warned me to stay away from the church custodian. A girl on my street said that the first night a man and woman get married, they sleep together in the same bed without any clothes on. Why would they do that? None of this made any sense.

I didn't know what hormones were but I certainly felt that something strange was going on in my body, doing something to my mind as well. It became hard to think about anything else and I knew all this kind of thinking was sinful. I would have to tell it all in confession. Ferreting through the information provided by the nuns on how to do confession, I came up with a way to confess while avoiding the gory details of my transgressions.

I rehearsed: "Bless me, Father, for I have sinned. It has been two weeks since my last confession."

That was the script, the opening, the easy part, but then I had to fess up. I'd have to tell how many times I had been "impure in thought," "impure alone," and/or "impure with others," something I could only dream about. This was the sanitized language I would use, and hope to get a priest that didn't ask questions. Actually, I soon learned, I could do more than hope. I could do what today would be called consumer research.

We had several priests in our large parish. They handled the commerce of confession in the church on Saturdays, hidden away in a small booth with three doors, seated behind the center door. Two lines of parishioners lined up in the aisle, waiting for the opportunity to enter one of the side doors, confess and be absolved from their sins, provided they faithfully carried out their penitence, the repetition of various prayers, the Our Father, the Hail Mary, and promised to try to not repeat the sins. The number of repetitions was based on the severity of the sins, though there was no precise scale. It was left to the priest to determine this.

We never knew for certain, at least not at first, which priest was behind which of the several doors available on any given Saturday. Some priests had a reputation for being harsh, punitive and, worse of all, inquisitive. Those were the ones we tried to avoid. As I chose a line and stood waiting, I watched to see who came out of the confessional. If it was a kid I knew I would try to find out which priest was in the box, looking for some sign, a wink, a nod, a whispered name, like spies passing on secrets. If it was a harsh priest, I would hop over to another line.

Which priest was the best to get was a constant source of discussion among us kids, and probably among

27

the adults as well. So, the Saturday confession was much like a game show as we took our chances and played off our best information and the odds of selecting the course of least embarrassment.

Walking home from confession, I always felt so good. I had a clean slate. If I were to die then, I would go directly to heaven, but it would have to happen soon. My slate would soon fill up again. But I didn't really want to die. Heaven seemed like a really cool place, but I wasn't sure there were boobs there.

Going Feral

We pleaded and pleaded and finally our parents gave in. We could pick one of the cute little kittens from the litter, complements of a family up the street, anxious to get rid of this new bounty of felines. We picked a snow-white one, a bright-eyed ball of cotton. We discussed names as we carried it down the street and into our house.

It was getting dark out as we set it down in our brightly lit kitchen. We made a bed of a cardboard box and old cloth. We watched in amazement as the little tongue lapped up warm milk.

It was mostly my little sister and I who did the pleading and begging, and were most interested in the new pet. Our older siblings were of an age that they were beginning to assert an independence, saving the begging and pleading for more important matters such as curfew times.

The kitchen led out to a labyrinth of narrow alleys, behind all the stores, bars and homes. During the day, it was a maze of delight. At one turn, there was a honey-suckle bush, good for a sweet drop of nectar if you knew how to pick the bud, pinch the base of the blossom and gently pull the pestle through the bottom. A golden drop would appear and grow, the taste like honey. At another there were concrete blocks to sit on, the remnants of some old foundation. The alley was too narrow and had too many turns for bicycles as it snaked past trash cans, fences and small back yards filled with interesting debris, but we spent much time there on foot.

At night, no one went there except the wild things. Lying on my bed, windows open in vain attempt for relief from the sweltering city heat, I would hear the strange and frightening shrieks of cats. The sounds were unworldly. I tried to picture what they looked like and what they were doing. One that had once been ours was out there somewhere. Our new kitten was a replacement, we reminded our parents, for one they had permitted us to adopt and raised from a little baby and was now lost to the lure of the alley. I couldn't understand why he would choose that dreadful place over the comfort and love we provided. Years later, when I started to experience my own desires, the quest for freedom, the draw of lust, it made more sense.

When the first cat started insisting on going out, scratching at the kitchen door, begging, pleading, we gave in. Mom just didn't want him damaging the door. We just wanted him to be happy. At first the excursions were brief and during the daylight hours. We would hear the scratching on the door when he returned and quickly let him back in. He started staying out longer, sometimes not returning till after dark. His stays at home got shorter. He took on an air of defiance and privilege. He was no longer cute. His grooming was poor. His look was wicked.

Then he stayed out overnight and came home with cuts and scratches. He wouldn't let us touch him, and we didn't much want to. Then he was out two days in a row, then three. We lost count. When he did come home he wanted food, demanding it be served up quickly, becoming more impatient with us as time went on.

We would hear the scratching at the door and open it. He would look us in the eye with a menacing appraisal, and then strut across the floor to the dish at the opposite wall. If the weather was cold he would linger and stretch his sinewy body near the heating vent. If we had offered him a cigarette, I think he would have taken it in his paw and expected a light. As time went on he visited less often. Summer nights I listened to the strange sounds of the alley and thought of him. Months went by without a visit and we concluded we would never see him again. The time of pleading for a new kitty had returned.

We watched the new little kitty closely as he began to settle there in the kitchen, just beginning to get comfortable in his new home. We were enjoying every cute little movement, when we heard the sound at the door, a menacing, demanding, scratching and thumping. One of us, I don't remember who, opened the door, and there he was, lean, mean, demonic, a creature of the night and of the darkest corner of life. He glared at us, looking each of us in the eye in a most demeaning manner. Then his gaze fixed on our new little kitten, who suddenly stopped lapping at the bowl.

His saunter across the room seemed to take forever. The kitty's eyes were wide with incomprehension at the figure coming his way. The old cat's head hung low and his eyes were now fixed to the floor. When he got to the dish he attacked, swatting the kitten away with a sudden flash of claws accompanied by a screeching hiss.

The kitty went flying, then slipping and sliding on the linoleum, seeking safety. The cat bent over and lapped up the milk. He turned and strolled back to the door. We opened it. Before stepping across the threshold, he gave us each a final look. In the moment, I was locked on his eyes. I saw depths of demons I could scarcely understand. Then he was gone. We never saw him again. I listened for him on summer nights, through the open bedroom window.

The Lost boy

Dad warned us. It was going to be very crowded on the subway. We needed to stay close together and hold hands. Hold hands? We'd rather eat worms. Though we were not yet in our teens, we felt much too old to be doing such a thing.

Dad was taking us, his three sons, to a baseball game at Connie Mack Stadium, home of the Philadelphia Phillies. We were thrilled at the opportunity to see our heroes of the diamond, live and in action. So perhaps we could at least stand close enough together to make it look like we were holding hands

The station was indeed crowded as we made our way through the turnstiles and onto the platform. When the train came, we were caught up in the rush of fans and made our way on. Or at least most of us did. As the doors closed and the train began to move away from the station, we realized that Danny was missing. Then, through the window, we saw him running alongside the train, a look of panic on his face. As our train pulled away, Chucky looked at us and said, "He wasn't such a bad kid after all."

But Dad was not about to write him off. He came up with a plan. We got off at the next station and he went to the man at the ticket booth. Dad told him what had happened and asked him to call back to the station where we got on, tell the ticket taker to find the kid on the platform, put him on the next train, and tell him to get off at the next station where we would be waiting for him. The man did so, but there was another problem. A big one. There was no kid on the platform. There was no one at all on the platform.

The look on my father's face was like none I had ever seen before as we tried to come to grips with the situation. Did he climb down onto the tracks? If so, he would likely get electrocuted or run over by the next train. Or maybe both. I thought of a recent cartoon I had seen of a coyote running at full speed and smashing into a wall he did not see coming. He flattened out like a pancake and slowly slid to the ground. Perhaps this was what happened to Danny when he got to the edge of the platform.

We stood on the empty platform looking to Dad for a solution. We could almost see his mind rushing along, an anguished expression on his face, wondering what happened to his son. Then another, almost empty train pulled into our station. Out stepped a tall, dark skinned man, impeccably dressed in a dapper suit and smart hat. He was holding Danny by the hand. He graciously handed him back to us.

We went on to the ballpark. But nothing that happened on the field that day could top the excitement of us getting there.

The Ransom of Pagan Babies

It was such a difficult decision. Sitting in Sister Agnes Marie's third grade classroom I clutched hard to my nickel as Franny Scanlon and Dominick Demoski worked their way up and down the aisles on the boy's side of the room with the tray of treats, one holding the tray while the other took the money. Margaret McGinley and Rita Massy worked the girl's side. They were the ones picked that day as a reward for some sort of exemplary behavior.

Sister Agnes Marie had just given us another lecture on being good Catholic children and the duty we have to do works of mercy. She told us how fortunate we were to be born in a free country and have families that cared for us, and to be blessed by the Lord, our God and Savior. She said that, in faraway places there were poor, suffering children who didn't have enough to eat or drink, much less a nickel to spend on treats. Even worse than being poor and hungry, these children were ignorant, which meant they didn't go to school, and had never been told about the Holy Trinity or been shown the path of Christianity. They weren't Catholic, so they could never get into heaven.

Pagans were heathens. They wouldn't burn forever and ever in hell after they died, since they didn't know what they were doing. They would go to Limbo, an in-between place where nothing ever happened. This was not an option for me, since I had been shown the path to everlasting life in heaven. If I chose to turn away from the path, I would go to hell. There was one thing worse than being a pagan, we were told, and that was being a fallen away Catholic.

I knew that before long I would be making my Confirmation and then receive the Eucharist, the body of Christ melting on my tongue. When hormones raged, my sins would pile up like sands upon the shore, to be cleansed away by Confession and penitence; then start to pile up again with each successive wave. It would occur to me that, unless I died on the way home from Confession, I'd end up in hell, or at least be doing some serious hard time in Purgatory. Sometimes I'd envy those pagan babies who never had to face the burning fires. I still have a hard time with reward and punishment.

Pagans didn't know that they shouldn't eat meat on Friday, or that they should give up something they liked during Lent. I thought this didn't matter much since they didn't have anything to give up and probably didn't have meat since there were no stores around where they lived to buy it, even if they did have money.

I thought of them, dirty and dressed in rags, in some hot and steamy jungle filled with insects and wild animals. They weren't the same color as us and they didn't speak our language, but they had souls just like us and they needed to be saved and baptized. We could help save them with our pennies and nickels.

Sister Agnes said that it was time for the annual campaign to ransom pagan babies and that our class would be competing with all the other classes to see which class could raise the most money and save the most babies. She kept tabs on the blackboard in chalk, four little sticks in a row. Then she would draw a line through them signifying a group of five. When we got to a certain number we had one whole baby and we got to give the kid a name. The first one would be a girl name, the second a boy and so on. Girls always got to go first. I thought about suggesting "Roy" for the first boy's name, in honor of my favorite cowboy, Roy Rogers. Then I remembered the rule that the name we picked had to be the name of a Saint. I didn't think there was ever a Saint Roy. I had trouble with rules. I never could figure out what I had to do to get to sell the treats. That would be cool.

I tried to picture how the actual transition of the ransom was done. In my mind, I saw our Monsignor Bower, a bald old priest with a pot belly, dressed in his long black cassock, carrying huge bags full of our nickels and pennies, struggling through the dense tropical jungle. Then he would meet a strange and nefarious heathen, scantily clad in filthy rags, and holding a baby. They would look at each other suspiciously. Then Monsignor Bower would hand over the bags of coins and quickly snatch the baby. I thought it would be a relief for him to have that light baby instead of the heavy coins to carry back through the jungle.

I wondered what he would do with the kid; probably give it to some nuns who would take care of it in a convent while they went about saving the kid's soul. Growing up in the care of nuns would be really horrible, I thought. I'd rather be raised by wolves. I wondered what the pagan guy did with all those coins. Maybe some pagan kids got some of it to buy treats, trekking miles through swamps to find a store. Maybe he bought more babies to ransom. Who knows. It's hard to figure out pagans.

The competition got fierce in the second week of the drive. Sister Mary Xavier's class was ahead of us by just one-half baby, and Sister Marie Adele's class was less than a baby behind. A lot was at stake, class pride and bragging rights at the convent. By the third week a good third of our blackboard was covered with chalk marks, lined up neatly like soldiers. We competed like horses in the derby, or our Phillies on the field.

I can't even remember which class won that year. I know my class did win at least one year. I do remember that day in school, Franny and Dominic coming down the aisle towards me, the nickel in my hand. I could spend it selfishly on a Hershey chocolate bar or soft pretzel, or I could help ransom one of those poor babies. Memory is tricky. Sometimes I remember things the way I wished they had happened. But I do believe that on that opening day of the Pagan Baby Drive, I acted like a true soldier of God. I seem to remember my empty stomach pleading noisily shortly after. I recall struggling to keep my eyes on Sister Agnes and my ears on the history lesson, but all I could think about was the dreamy heat of the afternoon sun, beaming in through the windows, and that doughy soft pretzel I could have had at snack time.

There were days when the choice was between the pretzel and the candy, with the babies running a distant third. All in all, I think I did my part, walking a delicate balance between feeding the flesh and feeding the soul. Later in life, in a cynical mood, I wondered if our cherished coins actually went to the convent wine fund. Perhaps it was just some gambling racket. But

I'd like to think that this was a sincere, guileless crusade to save children. Perhaps someday I will get a call or an email from one of those kids I saved, all grown up. He will thank me for the nickels and pennies I gave to save him. Maybe he will be rich now and offer to pay me back, or at least buy me a soft pretzel. Sounds crazy, but you never know.

Gotum, Gotum, Needum

He wanted to see mine and I wanted to see his. So, there in the school yard, this kid I did not know and I agreed to show each other what we had. From the bulging pocket of my pants I whipped mine out. He did the same. There they were, exposed for all to see. Other kids gathered around. It wasn't the first time I had done this, but it was the first time with a kid I did not know. I had no way to calculate what he would think of mine, what he might want and what he might offer in exchange. He grabbed mine and I grabbed his. We started flipping through each other's precious stack of baseball cards.

It is difficult to explain how important these cards were for us. They not only represented our heroes of the diamond, collected through endless hours of chewing stale bubblegum and spending our hard-earned pennies, each time with the hope that we would unwrap the pack and find a true gem, a Mickey Mantle, a Willy Mays, or a home-town great like Richie Ashburn. These cards became our currency. We traded them and gambled with them, flipping them and tossing them in various ways in games of skill and chance with hopes of winning the jackpot and becoming rich.

The cards were also educational. On the backs of them I learned all kinds of important historical facts. I learned that our ace, Robin Roberts, started three games in the last five days of the 1950 season, leading the Wiz Kids to an upset win over the Brooklyn Dodgers. That year he was the first 20-game-winner for the Phillies since Grover Cleveland Alexander in 1917.

I learned that Richie Ashburn, in the last game of that same year, threw Dodger runner, Carl Abrams out at home plate, preserving a 1-1 tie, setting the stage for Dick Sisler's pennant-clinching home run. None of this was in our school history books. Surely the pennant race of 1950 was as important as the war of 1812.

I also learned geography. Richie was born in Tilden, Nebraska. Chico Fernandez was born in a place called "Cuba". I even looked it up on a map in our geography book.

I had little inkling at the time that I would soon become cynical about our Phillies, as they struggled to stay out of last place for so many years of my youth. Years later I became convinced that two of our outfielders had clearly established a record that had never been mentioned or considered in all of the massive amount of baseball statistics. Bob Bowman and Harry (The Horse) Anderson hit more long fly balls to the warning track than any other two players in baseball history. It was amazing how they could calculate the distance at all the many ballparks around the country. And how they could adjust their swing for the wind. If they were just a foot off in either direction the ball would go over the fence for a homerun or be short of the warning track for a less dramatic routine fly.

But, on this day in the schoolyard, my hopes were high. We were nearing the end of the school year. I was too young to be jaded. Pitchers and catchers had already reported for spring training. Soon we would be hearing the call: "Play ball!"

"Gotum, Gotum, Needum" the strange boy began, singling out and declaring which cards he needed to complete his set. I followed suit. We separated out the ones we wanted.

Once that was settled, the difficult negotiation began. How many cards would I have to offer him for his Stan Lopata? Would he accept my doubles or would I have to give up a one-of- a -kind from my collection? What should I demand for my Ed Bouchee? We made a few easy transactions. Then it got down to some high-stakes decisions. Fortunately, the bell rang, signaling the end of recess, before we got in too far over our heads.

Family Gifts

With seven kids and limited resources, Christmas gift giving was a challenge for our family back when we were young. Mom and Dad somehow always managed to provide heaps of gifts for us, but it was certainly beyond our means for each of us to give each other gifts. So, Mom and Dad had us do a Pollyanna. At Thanksgiving, Mom would do the drawing of names and each of us was assigned one sib to buy a gift for. Who had whom was supposed to be a secret until the gifts were opened on Christmas morning. But some of us, mostly the girls in the family, saw secrecy as a challenge, or a contest to see who could figure out the matches before the gifts were opened.

Each of us kids also bought a gift for Mom and Dad, with money we got from Mom and Dad, who also funded our Pollyanna through allowance and chore payments. Though he gave us a lot of himself, Dad, like many men then and now, was not much into gift giving. He left that to Mom, but he had to get her a gift each year. Sometimes, on Christmas eve, he would ask one of us to run down to the corner drug store to buy a bottle of Jean Naté perfume for her.

Jean Naté was Mom's favorite perfume and her one luxury in life. The problem was that we all knew this, so she would often end up with several bottles of the foe-French concoction every Christmas. She got so much of it over the years, for her birthday as well as Christmas, that I suspected that, after she died, we would find a closet full of the stuff. But we did not. Perhaps, she managed to bury it all somewhere. I like to think that the lingering scents of lavender, jasmine, rose, carnation, lily of the valley, cedar, musk and sandalwood followed her into the afterlife. When I come across these scents now, in the fields and gardens of spring and summer, I like to think that Mom dropped them there for me. Fanciful thinking, I know. But 'tis the season for that.

Our parents are long gone, but the Pollyanna continues on. Over the years, spouses were added.

Death claimed some and others are no longer able to participate. Someday we and the Pollyanna will be gone. Nothing lasts forever. It took me many years to realize that the most precious gift we ever got was each other, crammed into that little row house in Philadelphia.

Games

Once upon a time kids made up their own games, which were played without batteries. There was no need for computer programmers because there were no computers. The games were passed on from child to child. They were modified and evolved over time in response to the changing environment. Materials and equipment were gathered with limited resources, and games developed based on what was available.

Growing up in Philly in the 1950's we played kick-the-can, one of the most primitive and minimalistic of games. It basically involved kicking a tin can down the street, one team kicking it one way, one team, the other. Any old can would work. It could be peas, corn, or beans. It made no difference. I suppose there was some danger to parked cars, and the possibility of injury from flying cans if the game became too exuberant, and the cans had some sharp edges since openers were not as refined as they are today, but I can't recall any injuries or damage to property. Today the cans would be much safer, but no kid would think of spending time kicking one down the street.

With "Tag" we didn't even need a can. It goes back to the 12th century and was named after the now extinct Tagonians from the island of Tago, which was destroyed by a US nuclear test as the bombardier looked back and shouted, "You're it!" I think it is still played somewhere in remote aboriginal cultures and suburbs of Milwaukee. It still has great influence in political and economic matters.

We used pimple balls and pinky balls for stick ball, box ball, wire ball and a game we called "chink". It was while playing that game that I got a real-life lesson in racial stereotypes. We spent more time playing chink than any other game, mainly because it was so easy and we could play it right out back in our alley. I thought the name came from rough edges of the wall we played on, made with cement block. We could play with any number of kids, even girls sometimes. We started by throwing the ball against the wall directly or on one bounce. The next player had to hit it back with an open hand directly or on one bounce. Like many hand ball type games, the action was fast and furious. If someone missed a certain number of times, usually three with a big group, he was out.

When we played games in the street, neighbors would often chase us away or call the cops. When we saw a cop car pull into our street, we would know the game was over, at least for a few hours. We got to know some of the cops. Some we could joke with but others were hard core.

One day, while we were playing chink in the alley, Mr. Schmidt popped out his back door and yelled at us to chase us away. We told him we were just playing chink, and he said he didn't want to hear about our racist games. Wow, it never occurred to me that this game we loved may have, somewhere along the line of time, acquired a name that was a derogatory term for the Chinese. I had heard the term used in such a way before, but never associated it with the game we played. Such ethnic and racial slurs were fairly common in our world, but I was taught to avoid them, and I did. This one caught me totally by surprise. I pictured a bunch of kids playing this game in China. Perhaps they brought it over with them to America.

One of the neighbors up the street was a big, tough, retired cop, who seemed to hate kids in general. He once confiscated the new football I got for Christmas when it strayed too close to his garage in the back alley. When Dad went up to get it back from him, we anticipated a brawl. Fortunately, that didn't happen. We got our ball back and life went on as usual.

The next year one of my buddies got a football for Christmas. We were playing with it in the street. He warned me not to kick it so close to the houses, but I did. It landed on the porch roof of that very same hostile neighbor. It was my mistake and my responsibility to get it back. But how?

His house was similar to ours, so I knew that the only way to get that ball was to go through his living room, up the stairs to the second floor, down the hall, into the front bedroom he shared with his wife, and climb through the bedroom window onto the roof of his porch. Wow! Fortunately, I had no time to think about it. My buddy was insistent. He wanted his ball back and he wanted it immediately!

I walked up to the house and knocked on the door, overcome with dread, hoping he wasn't home. The door opened and there he was. I fearfully, very

48

fearfully, explained the situation, bracing for his wrath. He looked at me without expression. He turned and ordered me to follow him. I tried not to look around as he led me up the stairs and into his bedroom. He opened the window. I climbed out, got the ball, thanked him, and hurried back out to the street.

That was it. To this day I cannot explain it. It was all over. Nothing more was ever said. Everything returned to normal. We went back to playing in the street. He went back to chasing us away and calling the cops on us.

Bunk Beds

My son doesn't want them anymore. He is all grown up and lives far away. He has a toddler son and a daughter on the way. If he decides to use bunk beds it would be easier to buy them locally. This makes sense, so I climb the ladder in the garage to lower the dissected pieces from their perch on the rafters. They have been nestled there for so many years. They will need a good cleaning to ready them for the garage sale. I must find or replace the hardware and figure out how to assemble the beds and fit in the matching dresser.

My closeness to the objects brought back memories of the many nights I spent tucking my son into bed at night, the songs and the stories. Often stray thoughts, gathered through the day, would find voice, as though his mind needed to dump them out before settling down to sleep. I can almost smell the smells and feel the softness of the bedclothes.

When I was a child, Dad bought bunk beds for his three boys, crowded into a small back bedroom in our little row house. The four girls had the slightly bigger front bedroom. The bunk beds were genuine Navy surplus, verified by the letters deeply and perfectly carved into the bedpost: USN. The wood was covered with a thick skin of caramel shellac. We watched in anticipation as Dad got one bed directly on top of the other, held in place by notches that, we were told, needed to be checked often to be sure they didn't slip. This added a hint of danger that made it even more exciting. The top bunk was the most coveted. The bottom was cave like and could be made more so by hanging a sheet or a blanket from the top bunk to totally conceal the entrance. Either bunk would be much better than the single bed along the opposite wall.

Dad set up a rotation so we would each get to sleep in each bed. Chuck, the oldest, would start out in the top bunk and Dan, next in line, would start in the bottom bunk. I think we were to rotate monthly, but it seemed like years before I got out of the single and into the bottom bunk. When I did I was thrilled. I would lie awake at night and imagine myself as a sailor in a boat at sea, some nights a huge battleship in the Atlantic Ocean, others a submarine in the Pacific.

Then one night my fantasy was interrupted by a loud thump. Dan had rolled out of the top bunk. He was unhurt and pleaded to keep his top spot. Dad rigged a board on the side of the top bed to box him in, but a few nights later he managed to fall to the floor again. He pleaded again and dad reinforced the fall barrier. During this time dad was repapering our bedroom, stripping off the old wallpaper and hanging new paper, boy-paper with cowboys, I think. This was before the days of self-stick paper and the job was a messy venture, with buckets of paste and lots of waste gathered at the end of the day into a forty-gallon barrel next to the bunks. One night there was a thud and a screech. Dad came running and turned on the light. Dan had fallen head-first into the waste barrel, his feet sticking out and flailing. His time in the top buck had come to a dramatic end.

I got to move up and Dan had to move down. Dan was never hurt when he fell from the top bunk, but a few weeks later he fell out of the bottom bunk and broke his collar bone. I don't remember what happened to the rotation after that. It got less important to us as the novelty wore off and we got older. I don't remember when the beds left the house, probably sometime after I did. I wonder what other kids may have slept in them afterwards and what their experiences were like. I wonder what kids might get to use my son's bunk beds.

Siblicide

As much as I admired my older brothers and wanted to be like them, there were times when I wanted them out of my life. They had their own friends and usually didn't want a little brother hanging around them. When they did turn their attention to me it was usually to tease me. I remember one time Chucky got me so angry that I lost all control. I went into a rage and flung myself at him, swinging, kicking and screaming. Even when Mom came between us it took quite a while for her to calm me down. I don't remember the detail of the exchange, but I do remember what really popped my cork. It was that snide, demonic snicker he flashed at me.

Back then I felt that there was no way I could be the equal of my brothers ever, in any way. They seemed so smart, athletic and popular. Chucky was captain of the safety squad in grade school. He got to wear a really cool, white belt-like sash that went around his waist, across his chest and over his shoulder, like the bullet belt of the Mexican banditos I saw on TV. He even had a badge. I'd watch in amazement as he would stand on the corner as school let out and stretch out his arms. All the kids, the girls in their uniforms and the boys in their white shirts and school ties, had to wait on the corner until my brother dropped his arms and permitted them to cross the street – what power! He made the baseball team and even was picked to go to a summer camp once. He seemed invincible.

When he ended up in the hospital with a ruptured appendix I did not understand how serious this was. I thought of hospitals as places people go to get better. One day we walked home from school for lunch as usual. Mom and dad were at the hospital with Chucky. Mom had arranged for us to get lunch on our own. A knock came to the door and it was our parish monsignor, who we had only seen when he did a mass. To have him come to our door was a shock, to say the least. I thought that we were in big trouble and began searching my conscience for what I may have done that could be so bad that it required his attention. I was both relieved and perplexed when he addressed us in a friendly manner. Then he asked about our brother, Charles. He urged us to pray for him and had us all kneel so he could give us his blessing.

The monsignor's visit made me realize that my brother was in very serious condition and could die, which was much more likely to happen from such an ailment back then in the 1950's than it is today. I just could not imagine what it would be like to not have him around, not on the corner as captain of the safeties, not running around with his buddies, not picking on me. This was not a pleasant picture. For the first time ever, I worried about my brother.

Now we live far away from each other and don't get to visit often. He went from Chucky to Chuck sometime in his adolescence when my sister, Ann, decided it was time he had a grown-up name. When we do get together, we always have a pleasant time and we agree about most things. When we don't, I am always right and he is always wrong, just like that time long ago that I went into a rage and wanted to kill him, over something I can't remember, that time I don't need to talk about anymore because I got it out of my system.

Once I visited the Galapagos Islands and saw Nazca Boobies. Pregnant females of this bird species lay and hatch two eggs. Soon after birth, one of the young attacks the other and kills it. The momma bird just watches this and does not intervene at all. Ornithologists say this is a necessary form of obligatory siblicide. The momma bird has too few resources to support both of her chicks. The stronger one wins out, assuring continuation of the species. Our mom had very few resources to support her large brood. I'm sure glad she wasn't a Nazca Booby.

Potato Wall

Necessity is the mother of invention. I've heard this said many time and I'm sure you have also. It was certainly the case this night. We had to do something with the cold mashed potatoes staring at us from our supper plates. Having finished eating and growing tired of our antics, Mom and Dad were in the living room. We had to finish all the food on our plates before we could leave the table.

"Think of all the poor starving children in China who would love to have your food"

We told Mom we would be happy to scrape our plates into a box and send it to those kids, but she was not amused. We were doing more talking and fooling around than eating and now the food was cold, making it even harder for us to eat. Having lived through the Great Depression, our parents were intolerant of waste. Every morsel of food on the plate must be consumed. And so, we sat, the seven of us, and talked and laughed and shuffled the food around on our plates.

We tried the trick we often used in such situations, reciting a verse:

"Order in the court house. The monkey wants to speak. No talking, no laughing, no showing your teeth. One, two, three."

The first kid who cracked and did any of those things was ridiculed for being the monkey. It was so difficult. It took a lot of concentration and self-control not to let out a snicker or a giggle. It didn't take long for one of us to break.

And then it happened. We could almost see the light come on in Danny's head. His eyes got bigger and he silently stared out the back door. Beyond it was a short staircase that led down to a very small yard. Beyond the yard was a narrow alley and then a large brick wall, the side of the home of Mr. Louie Roth. His house was the first of a row of houses that faced Ashedale Street, which was around the corner from our house. He lived alone, smoked big cigars out front after supper, and looked a lot like Popeye.

Danny loaded a big glob of the cold potatoes on his fork and headed out the screen door. At the top of the stairs he flung the fork like a catapult. The glob shot all the way to the wall, hit it with a splat and stuck. We looked at each other in amazement. A primal excitement ran through us. It was a genuine Eureka Moment.

When Sir Isaac Newton saw an apple fall from a tree he instantly connected the thoughts in his head to complete his theory of gravitation. Isaac had his apple and Danny had his potato. Gravity was certainly a factor when Danny flung the potatoes. So, there we have it: a direct connection between my brother, Daniel Cooney, and the great scientist, Sir Isaac Newton. And for both of them, it was a moment and spontaneous inspiration.

Each of us at the table had to give it a try. We were thrilled at how we were able to do this, competing to see who could get a glob highest on the wall. We had so much fun that we did this again and again, over many nights of mashed potato meals. Somehow, we managed to keep this activity a complete secret from our parents and our friends. The wall became speckled with the white globs. They just stuck and stayed. None of those globs ever seemed to fall off. We would steal furtive glances at the wall when we were out playing with friend, and long, prideful looks when we were alone. No one else ever seemed to notice.

Now, so many years later, I'm still amazed that we managed to keep this great achievement from the rest of the world. Perhaps we could have used the knowledge we gained about the interface of wall and potato for the betterment of humanity, but we never thought of that at the time.

Perhaps the wall and the potatoes are still there today. Maybe I could organize a scientific expedition back to the old Olney neighborhood to see. If the wall is still there the glops may still be there also. If the globs are gone we certainly should be able to detect some traces of the potatoes with the latest scientific equipment. Gathering the data, we could compute the trajectory of each shot and, using advanced analytics, develop some important insight into the nature of brick and vegetable.

But probably that won't happen.

Twirling

"Stop it before you kill somebody" yelled Chucky.

Charlotte was practicing her baton twirling again in the living room, where my two brothers and I were busy with more important matters. Chucky, on the sofa, was reading a sports magazine. Danny, in the old stuffed chair, had his nose in Mad Magazine. I was stretched out on the floor in front of the TV trying to concentrate on the what was most important this Saturday morning: watching cartoons.

This was an often-repeated scene. Our oldest sister, Helen, twirled her way through Little Flower High School (AKA The weed) and so did sister Ann, the next in line. Now it was Charlotte's turn. She stood facing the large mirror on the wall, beginning slowly, her arm outstretched in front of her. Effortlessly the heavy metal baton seemed to turn on its own, as if powered by some silent internal engine. It picked up speed and Charlotte, gaining confidence transferred the whirling dervish from one hand to another, then back again, then behind her back, then under her high kicking leg. Now things were truly getting dangerous. Surely no lamp, knick-knack, window or person was safe.

If she had been outside she would now be tossing the rotating stick high in the air, completing a full turn of her body, and catching it again without the slightest hesitation of body or baton rotation. At least this is how in was supposed to work. But to get to that state of perfection required much practice. At times things would suddenly go horribly amiss. All at once, and without the slightest notice, the baton would free itself of its prescribed orbit and fly at top speed in a totally unpredictable direction. At other times, it would simply drop to the ground harmlessly, as though it had just gotten tired and given up.

My sisters would seldom give up. They had to practice and practice if they wanted to get into the fife and bugle corps or the color guard. With lots of hard work, a bright smile and a generous amount of the elusive quality of cuteness a girl might achieve the very pinnacle of success. She might actually be the one girl chosen to be the majorette, and lead the marching band. In the heady, post war years of the 1950's the aspirations of youth in our community tended to revolve around sports and patriotic pageantry. With enough effort, any boy might score the winning goal and become president of the United States. Any girl, endowed with the right physical characteristics, might lead the parade, become a stenographer, and raise a healthy and happy family.

"Get out of here with that damn thing!" Danny joined the fray.

He had crossed a line. We were not allowed to use curse words. Charlotte just went on with her twirling. She knew she could not use this infraction against Danny. She too, had crossed a line. She was not supposed to be practicing in the living room. But how else could she see herself and practice her smile as well as her dexterity? Outside she had to rely on the fuzzy reflections from the windows of parked cars along the curb, and store windows up the block. Storeowners were as quick to chase off baton twirlers as they were ball throwers.

My sisters always insisted that twirling was a perfectly safe activity. Even years later, as fully grown and rational adults, they insist that the rubber tips on each end prevented any possible harm. The long history of shattered glass and damaged bodies must certainly be the result of poor manufacturing and people just being in the wrong place at the wrong time. This rubber clings like the tightest of skins to the round, weighted ends of the baton and is the hardest rubber ever invented. Charlotte's was studded with little glass pellets to make the ends sparkle like diamonds. I truly believe that certain inanimate objects are out to get people. The double-edged razor blade of this era is a prime example. At rest the baton is an elegant, appealing and harmless object. It is also alluring. It is nearly impossible for boy or girl to see such an object and resist the temptation to pick it up and use it for some purpose. If not twirled, it can be swung like a bat. And bats beg to strike at something. The result is often painful.

I took delight in the rising agitation of my two older brothers. Too often they took delight in agitating me. It was so nice to see them being bothered, even if it meant that I had to also be in the danger zone. I imagined the baton flying loose and smashing Danny or Chucky squarely in the jaw. This gave me so much pleasure that I was certain I must have just committed a sin. I was learning all about sin in school. It was one of Sister Mary Agnes's favorite topics. I thought my way through the Ten Commandments. "Thou shalt not take pleasure in seeing thy brother get hit by a baton" was not listed. But I knew that most of my sins were not covered in the big ten. I never tried to put a cover on my neighbor's wife and was certain that I would never have any interest in doing so. But sin was much more complicated than that.

There are mortal sins and venial sins. The three things necessary to make a sin mortal (the really bad kind) are grievous matter, sufficient reflection and full consent of the will. Certainly, getting hit in the face by a baton was a serious matter. Unlike the cartoons, my brother would not just be knocked over and see stars and little birds circling around in his head for a while. There would probably be lots of blood and broken bones and a trip to the hospital. Then I would never get to see the rest of Howdy Doody. Missing the show would surely be a serious matter.

The pleasurable thought I had of my brothers getting hit by the baton just popped into my head, so I did not give it sufficient reflection. That's what I was doing now. Perhaps if I said a Hail Mary and asked God for help, this evil pleasure would go away.

The most sinful person I knew was classmate Joey Corbin. Joey knew words I had never heard and seemed to be an expert on something called sex. He called our teacher Sister Mary Anus. This was a big, big sin since she was married to God. Joey had to tell me what an anus was. He never seemed to worry about sufficient reflection, only getting caught. He told me about things men and women did that were so crazy and disgusting that they could not possibly be true.

Still, I found myself thinking a lot about things Joey said.

Maybe the baton would fly loose, crash through the Venetian blinds and the window and hit the mailman just as he started to stick the bills through the little slot in the door. Maybe it would smash the goldfish bowl. Whatever it did, I knew there was only one way this could end. Since Chucky and Danny yelled at her, Charlotte would certainly keep twirling until she lost control.

Suddenly I was seized with real fear. What if it smashed the TV screen! No other possibility could be more devastating than that. Could I go on living without the Mickey Mouse Club, Lassie, Superman and all those wonderful cartoons? This thought spurred me to action. I chose one of the most powerful weapons in my arsenal. I started whining. This was not just any whine. I poured my whole heart and soul into the mother of all whines. It was so loud that it brought a response from mom in the kitchen. "What's going on in there?"

My siblings were eager to explain. The problem was either that Charlotte was attacking us with a deadly weapon, or Danny was cursing. Truth is so often dependent on your point of view. Exaggeration is used

64

to enlighten rather than misguide. At least that is often the hope and the reasoning of the seriously offended. The cacophony that followed did more to obscure than reveal the facts, but it did have one desirable effect. The baton twirling came to a peaceful end, and it was all thanks to me. I had saved the family from disaster. I knew better than to expect the praise and gratitude from my siblings that I so richly deserved. I knew from watching TV that true heroes do not act for recognition. The gallant are motivated by the burning desire to do good and make the world a better place.

My siblings each stalked off to separate corners of the house, and I was left alone with what was left of Howdy Doody. I missed much of the show, but I was perfectly content. Today I had done my part to make the world a better place.

Danny Had a DA

My brother, Danny, had a DA, so I wanted one too. He was older than I was and smarter and cooler. I knew I would never be as old as he or as smart, but maybe I could be as cool.

We stood in front of the bathroom mirror, the morning of the first day at our new school. I watched as he dipped his fingers into the jar of Vaseline and rubbed it into is hair. He combed it straight back and then down on the sides. Then he combed the sides back so they came together at a point that did indeed look like the rear end of a duck. I copied him stroke for stroke. We finished up with the pompadour. It had to be just right, like Elvis's or Bobby Darin's.

Danny made it clear that I should not tell mom or the nuns at school that it was a DA. They would not like hearing the "a" word and would be disgusted that we would want to make our heads look like an anatomically correct water fowl. I should just tell them that it is a popular hair style and try to change the topic. We were boys from the big city attending school in the foothills of the Poconos, in the land of the Pennsylvania Dutch, where Dad had taken a job managing a hospital laundry. We lived there for just a year. We had no idea how our cultures would clash, and how strange we would look to the country kids. We just wanted to be accepted and were totally unaware of what that would take in such a close-knit community.

It was a difficult year for Danny. He won a regional school essay contest and advanced to the final competition. If he won that next level, he would get admission and free tuition to an elite Catholic High School. He was given a topic: *Why do only Catholics get into heaven?* He didn't believe that and refused to write the essay. He had a Jewish friend back in Philly who seemed certainly deserving of a spot within the pearly gates. The nun was furious. Not only was it a matter of faith, but bragging rights at the convent were at stake. She kept him in at recess, making him sit at his desk with a pencil and blank sheets of paper. That went on for several days without conversion, so she began to humiliate him in front of the class, perpetuating the stereotype of the undesirable outsider.

Finally, Dad was called at work and asked to come to the school to discuss the problem. He left his job and came to the school. He heard the complaint and talked to Danny. He told the nuns that Danny would not write the essay because he didn't believe that only Catholics can get into heaven. That was that.

I didn't know about this till many years later. Danny didn't share his thoughts and experiences with me much when we were kids. Our relationship was mostly based on insults. He might say "If you had another brain cell it would be lonely." I might respond, "If brains were dynamite you wouldn't have enough to blow your nose."

Just a few years before he died he made a point of telling me about the essay contest. It seemed important to him to share this formative event in his life. One of the last times I saw him he was in a nursing home. I had just come from visiting another nursing home that seemed much better and was willing to have Dan transfer there. When I saw him, I said "Dan, I have good news". He said, "You're leaving town?" Some things never change. But many things do and did for us over the years, in ways we could hardly imagine.

But back then, on that first day of school, so long ago, in front of the bathroom mirror we were just two ducks looking for a tranquil pond.

By the Sea

I checked the thermometer on the kitchen wall every five minutes, pleading with the mercury to rise to the magic number. My sister, Charlotte, had promised to take me and my younger sister, Kathy, to the Jersey shore if the temperature got to eighty degrees. It seemed reluctant to do so on this Saturday morning in late spring. I so wanted to be on the beach, body-surfing the day away after a hard year of elementary school. It had to get to eighty before it got too late to make the trip of an hour and a half or so from Philly.

Some places in the world folks go "to the beach" or "to the seaside." In Philly, we never did that. We went "down the shore," to Margate, Brigantine, Atlantic City, Wildwood or Cape May. There we would claim a spot of sand, stretch out our blankets, slab on our suntan lotion and have at it, going about the business of recreating and relaxing. We kids had no time for the latter. Relaxing was the furthest thing on our minds as we went about the business of swimming, playing on the beach and walking the boardwalk in search of adventure, cotton candy, salt water taffy and cheap thrills.

When we got older, the shore beckoned us with the lure of the bars and nightclubs, bustling with the possibility of linking up with someone special, for a night, a summer or lifetime. But for now, it was all about the waves. I loved how I could make my body a board, linking my thumbs together, standing, back to the ocean, hip deep in the surf, looking over my shoulder, watching for the perfect wave, reading it, getting into position, being in the perfect position for when it broke, pushing off and riding it in till my belly met the sand. Inevitably we would come home with burnt skin and the burning desire to go again.

As luck would have it, the thermometer reached eighty degrees in the nick of time. We eagerly jumped into the fabulous Ford convertible Charlotte and sister Ann owned. The two of them in the front and Kathy and I in the back. The car was white, with matching white skirts covering the back wheels and a continental kit extending from the back, holding the spare tire in a matching white cover. It had lots of glistening chrome. We cruised up the boulevard and crossed the mighty Delaware River on the Tacony Palmyra Bridge. It was hard to imagine life getting much better than this.

We arrived at the beach in time to get in a lot of body surfing, then we were off for ice cream. Then our older sisters decided to drop by a club that was connected to a bowling alley. They gave us money to go bowling. They went to the club, where they could watch us through a window. We had the entire place to ourselves. There was no one else bowling. When we completed a game, we were given money to play again. This happened several times. Charlotte and Ann were having a good time at the club and had met a couple of guys. When they finally decided to leave, we stepped outside, Ann and Charlotte with the two guys. At the curb were two shiny, new sports cars that the two guys owned. I asked my sisters which one they like best. They blushed. It wasn't till many years later that they told me they thought I was asking about the guys.

The Last Hug

This is a story about a boy, a dog and a hug. Any tale containing these elements runs the risk of being excessively sentimental or down-right maudlin. I fervently strive to avoid such sentiment, considering it in poor taste. I was bred to see it as unmanly. I grew up in a world that taught boys to be tough. I doubt that, in this regard, the world is much different today. To cry or show any sign of weakness was met with scorn and contempt by other kids. It was the sharpest of insults to call a boy a baby, or worst yet sissy.

My two older brothers (the eldest dubbed "Tuffy" by dad) were the fiercest family guardians of this creed, quick to pounce on my slightest transgression. Through my early years, I learned of several things I needed to be careful about in order to be truly male. For instance, it was important to avoid any prolonged interaction with my sisters. The danger was that I might inadvertently, or by subversive female intent, fall into some exchange or activity which was not sufficiently male. It was important that I avoid too close an attachment to mom so that I not be considered a momma's boy. This required avoiding her hugs as much as possible.

Now mom's hugs were often hard to avoid. They were by no means soft and gentle, but strong, German hugs. Often, they came with little warning. Suddenly you were engulfed by two arms of steel, and caught in an embrace that spoke of generations. It had the feel of years of joys and sorrows, and the warmth of survival. It was possessive and caring, true and loving. Sometimes, for the very young, it was a prelude to a bounce upon her knee, which was accompanied by an odd verse:

"Sucker, sucker rider,
went to catch a spider,
fell in the green-a-grass

sixteen-a-bookernocker
Fell in the soot
Mocker rider BOOM!"

The words were silly, yet magical. Many years later, when I was an adult, I heard this verse in German, from a woman who bounced a child on her knee. The actual translation to English was totally different in content, but just as silly. Mom's version captured the sound of the German words, rather than the meaning. The effect on the child was always the same as the knee came down at the end. How many generations of children experienced this thrill before me?

Well, it came to pass that, at the time of this story (Circa 1959), I was about 12 years old, on the verge of a period of my life that would be ruled by raging hormones. Each day after school I was greeted at home by a dog and an empty living room. Seldom in our family of nine did total possession of the living room occur, yet I had this situation to look forward to at the end of each and every school day. Brother Danny was now in high school, and like my other older siblings (off at school or jobs), did not get home until much later, shortly before dad. Mom was working on the corner as a crossing guard. Younger sister Kathy was usually home, but off on her own somewhere.

To make things even better, I had a high spirited young dog just waiting for some fun. We two mutts would chase each other and wrestle furiously, pushing ourselves to the brink before collapsing, totally spent, on the sofa in front of the TV. As I watched the tube, the dog would sleep with his head or half his body in my lap. I would try my best to be perfectly still as long as I could, so that I would not disturb him. Mom would come home next, and find us in quiet repose, with little hint of the preceding mayhem.

One day I came home and the dog was gone. This was not the first time he had somehow managed to get out in the afternoon and roam the city streets, but this time was different. Usually I would head out the back door and up the alley and find him. This time, as I started up the alley, some neighbor kids came with the news that he had been struck by a car. I ran up the alley in a daze. When I got to the end, where the alley meets the street, there was a police car with flashing lights. It was over. The dog was dead and his body had been removed. The cop was in the car, looking down and writing something into a book. Kids who had been on the scene were now gathering around me. I turned and started back down the alley. All around me was the teeming life of the city, but it seemed apart from me. I was in some timeless space between layers of truth. Finally, I was at my own back door.

The smell of supper was in the air. I could hear that Kathy, Chucky and Danny were in the house. I looked at mom and fell into her open arms, completely untethered from any societal restrictions. We found a chair and I cried unabashedly in her strong warmth.

Remembrance is like a vision, often striking with clarity unaffected by years. Even today, so many years later, that time in her arms is crystal clear. The aroma of the meal on the stove, the texture of the light from the old, chipped chandelier, the beating of my mother's heart and the pulse of this family moment come back to me vividly. We did not speak, but her arms told me that I could stay as long as needed. I was being comforted by a professional. I have no idea how long this lasted. To me it was timeless. I gradually pulled myself together enough to be concerned about what my brothers would say. Certainly, I had violated every known, and yet to be discovered code of male conduct. Not only had I hugged, but I displayed extreme and shameless weakness.

To my utter amazement, no one spoke a word nor gave the slightest gesture of rebuke. I don't believe another word was said to me about the dog. After all these years, I can't even recall the dog's name, but I will never forget that hug. This is not the last hug I ever shared with mom, but it was the last of my childhood. I was determined, like children everywhere, even those without big brothers, to fledge and then fly away. As an adult, I was fortunate to share many hugs with mom. The strong arms were still there, but it was altogether a different experience.

Easy Riders

It was a moment like none other in my life. At the time, I had no idea how meaningful it was, and how it would resonate throughout the years. I was eleven years old and, awaking from a deep slumber, crawled down from the upper bunk bed in the back bedroom I shared with my two older brothers. I stood there, looking out the window, up the alley of our Philadelphia row home. The brilliant morning sun gleamed off the windows to one side and cast shadows on the other. I was alone in the room and felt a relief and contentment I have often tried to recapture.

This was the first morning of summer vacation from school. It had been a brutal school year, but now it was over, and I was free, completely free. I had three months to do as I pleased. The feeling was exquisite.

We were free-range kids back then, in the late 1950's. No demands on us other than being home for dinner, and a few easy chores. I didn't realize it then, but this would be the last time I had such freedom. The following year I would become a paper boy, delivering the Philadelphia Bulletin on my bicycle. I would earn money by mowing lawns (reel mower) and taking out the trash at the corner drug store, starting off a chain of work, unbroken for most of my life. Hormones would kick in, setting off intense feelings and emotions I could hardly control. I would never have such a summer, such a moment, such a day again.

Mom came into the room and began assessing my readiness for the months ahead. She had me try on pants to see if they fit, pulling and poking. I remember feeling I was getting too old for such invasion of my privacy. I needed sneakers. Mom wanted to buy me the cheap Sears brand. I think they were eight dollars. I wanted the Chuck Taylor Converse All Stars. I think they were twelve dollars, way too expensive for Mom. I told her she could get me the Sears brand, but they would not last me through the summer, maybe two weeks at best.

I went down stairs, ate some cereal and headed out the back door. I climbed on my bike, my trusty steed. One of the Hatch boys appeared on his bike. He was a year or two younger than I was and not a close friend, but he was ready and so was I. Mrs. Hatch hatched a lot of Hatches. I think this one was Jimmy. He was a quiet kid. I took off and he followed.

Our bikes were old and well worn, but reliable. We mostly put them together ourselves, salvaging and swapping old parts and patching tire tubes till they were more patch than tube. No one had gears on their bikes. The brakes were on the pedals. Fortunately, the landscape was flat. We pedaled and pedaled, up Loretto Avenue where I lived, for several blocks, farther than we had ever gone before. Then we just kept going. We didn't talk much. We didn't have to. We went all the way to Cottman Avenue before taking a stop. We looked at each other and decide to go on. We went east on Cottman to the Roosevelt Boulevard, crossed it and then rode north all the way to the Pennypack Circle, then into Pennypack Park. Then we rode back to the boulevard, which is Interstate 1, and peddled north to New York City. Then we continued on to Boston.

Okay, we didn't really do some of that. But we could have if we wanted, and hadn't gotten tired and hungry. I'm certain we made it to Cottman Avenue, a distance of about a hundred and two miles (give or take a hundred). We had no destination in mind when we left, but now we just wanted to get back home. We got back in time for dinner and no one even knew we were gone. Mom bought me the cheap Sears sneakers and I wore them out in two weeks without really trying, playing games in the concrete alleys and on the asphalt streets. Then she bought me my first pair of the much-coveted Chuck Taylor Converse All Stars.

That day came back to me vividly over fifty years later, on the day I retired from the world of employment. I tried to recapture the wonderful feeling of freedom I felt looking out my bedroom window that morning, but I couldn't quite get there. Too many years, too many experiences and responsibilities got in the way. I came as close as I could.

I still have a bicycle and ride it from time to time. Back in the day no one over 16, the age one could acquire a license to drive a car, would ever consider riding a bicycle. Some things do change for the better. Some moments from the past linger below the surface of our consciousness and, conjured up by sheer will power or erupting without consent, bring us back to who we were. Some are moments of obvious power: births, deaths, times of jubilation and tragedy.

But sometimes moments of seemingly little consequence, when nothing much happens, like that time in my bedroom so long ago, sprout up and flower, providing cherished moments of sheer pleasure.

Winter Crime Report
A tale of two snowballs

I don't know what the statute of limitations is for the crime I am about to report, but I think I'm safe. It happened a long time ago, back around 1959, just off the Oxford Circle in Northeast Philly. Just in case, I have changed the names of some of the main characters to protect the guilty.

When Merv Melrose purchased the drug store at the corner of Oxford and Loretto from the Rachmel brothers one of the first things he did was take out the phone booths inside the store. They took up valuable space and he got no income from them. All those nickels and dimes went to Ma Bell. He had a new one put outside to compensate. It was all glass and aluminum, the standard issue, not at all as charming or comfortable as the old wood and glass ones, but it sure did work for us, me and my buddies who would hang out on the corner and wait for the phone to ring.

We gave all the girls we met the phone booth number and hung out there waiting for a call. It was our semi-private hotline to a world of potential sexual ecstasy, never fulfilled but always hopeful. We did get calls, but the conversations, though extensive at times, never were in any way sexually explicit. While we flirted on the border, the slightest misstep would end abruptly with a hang up. That happened often, particularly when Timmy got to the phone first, as he usually did. He was quick and especially tuned in to the ring tone, with a vigor and determination that would make Pavlov's dogs envious. He was primal and instinctive, like a rat sensing cheese.

While we hung out we found other activities to occupy our time. In winter, when there was snow, there was the irresistible draw of the snowball, the perfect object for the release of our hormonal-driven hostilities and creativities. The W bus was an easy and obvious target, so big and easy to hit as it slowed and stopped at the corner. It was a bit of fun to see the passengers flinch when we got one right on a window, but not much of a challenge.

I believe it was just the Sunday before the crime that I smacked Pete O'Toole on the head. He was headed to church, full of himself as usual, dressed up in his go-to-mass suit and wearing earmuffs of all things. None of the cool guys wore earmuffs back then. He seemed to be actually prancing, with every stride saying, "Look at me."

I did. He was way across the intersection when I utter those words that so often lead to disaster: "Watch this." I threw my perfectly formed snowball as high and as far as I could, with no expectation at all that I would actually do what I claimed, hitting Petey on the top of his head. It did, coming down directly on top of him and knocking off his earmuffs. I was almost as stunned as he was. He may never had known what had happened if it wasn't for Timmy, who started laughing loudly and profusely, doubled over with laughter.

Pete, who was much bigger and stronger that we were, heard the laughter and came running towards us like an angry bull. He started plummeting Timmy, who kept trying to tell him that he didn't do it, I did. I stood there motionless at first, trying to devise some appropriate exit from the scene. Much to my relief Pete wasn't buying what Timmy was saying. It seemed the laughter was far worse than the actual assault.

So, about a week later, getting back to the crime, we were standing on the corner with snow balls when Timmy says, "Watch this". He then hurls his snowball, which was really more of an ice ball, at a passing cop car. As luck would have it, the cop, for some inexplicable reason, had his window down. Timmy's icy ball hit the cop right on the side of his head, knocking off his hat. We wasted no time. I don't think either of us ever ran so fast. My house was just down the alley. Timmy's house was many streets away. I ran into the basement in the back of our house and bolted the door shut. Timmy pounded on the door but I would not let him in. At the very least, I thought, I would be an accessory to the crime. I pictured cops surrounding the house and shouting through bullhorns: "Come out with your hands up." I saw what they do on TV. I didn't want to go to jail. I didn't want to bring this down on my family.

Ok, so I'm not real proud of this. It's been over fifty years and I still wonder if I did the right thing. At the time, I thought I'd never see Timmy again. I pictured him gunned down in an alley or arrested and interrogated about the crime. Would he rat me out? So, what would you have done? Was I wrong to lock him out? When he showed up again several days later his relief that he had not been caught was far greater than his anger at me. We kept a low profile in the neighborhood for several weeks before returning to the corner, the scene of the crime. Even then, we cautiously watched for cop cars.

Looking back, I long for the pleasure of the release of a snowball from my adolescent hand, that perfect orb created by a boy from the flakes of heaven, hurled with hopes and intents and endless possibilities, into the frosty air. As a child, you never know where it or you will land. That day I never would have thought that Timmy would grow up to be a cop. He did.

The Best Hot Dog Ever

It was hot and humid and I was sitting in the bleachers at Connie Mack Stadium watching the Phillies, who were about to lose another game. They did that a lot when I was growing up in Philadelphia in the 1950's. I was there with my dad and my two older brothers.

Back then we had no air conditioning, so the fans were hot and sweaty by the time they got to this afternoon game. Even more so were the vendors who spent the game climbing up and down steep aisles carrying heavy containers of beer, peanuts, Cracker

Jack, cotton candy, ice cream and hot dogs. They were always working the crowd, shouting out what they had to offer. The cotton candy guys (yes, all the vendors were male) had it easy, I thought, carrying so light a load. It seemed that they were the younger guys. That didn't seem fair. I thought the older guys should get the lighter stuff to carry. Maybe they didn't trust the young guys with the heavy stuff. Maybe they had to prove themselves worthy.

Some vendors tried to engage the fans in a witty banter, loaded with stale jokes, in an effort to draw attention from the action on the field. In those sad days of the franchise it was not difficult.

Money flowed from hand to hand down the row to the vendor and the goods flowed hand to hand to the fans. Many factors affected the speed of the flow, chief among them were alcohol consumption and events on the field, but the exchange always seemed to work out. The goods were delivered and money got transferred successfully.

Now hot dogs at the ballpark back then were not subject to the level of government oversight they are today, and I don't think they had the preservatives used today. They were beef, or some facsimile thereof, and swam in vats of hot liquid the vendors carried strapped around their shoulders as they climbed up and down the various sections of the stadium. Some of those dogs may have been in those same vats for several days, I thought. The aging may have enhanced their flavor

On this day, I stood in the aisle looking up at the vendor. He was heavy and loud, spitting out booming enticements, "Hot dog here! Who'll have a hot dog?"

Perspiration dripped from his grisly face. Clouds of spittle projected from his mouth with every word. The lid to the dogs was open so the vat caught much of this. His hands prepared my hotdog as his eyes continued to scan the crowd looking for the next sale.

He was easily twice my size. I was just a kid. I wasn't sure he heard my order for one with sauerkraut and mustard, so I repeated it. That was a mistake. He gave me a look that said "Stop bothering me kid." My order was in process. The aroma steaming out of the hot vat was splendid. He dipped his hand into the vat and plucked out a dog with his tongs and put it on the bun he had waiting in his other hand. Then he opened the vat with the sauerkraut and I experience an aroma like none other. I wanted to lean my head into the vat and suck up all I could of it. There are no words to describe it. It was primordial, conjuring up the toil of generations past, the goodness of the fermented, ancient earth. I was dazed. By the time I came to my senses I realized that I had the delightful concoction in one hand and my change in the other. The vendor was climbing back up the aisle, shouting, dripping and spitting. I took a bite and I was gone again.

There are rare moments in life when time seems to stand still and all the senses are focused and sparkling at once. All worries and concerns are vanquished. Just then I heard the crack of a bat and the fans rose to their feet with joyful anticipation. The ball shot high into the sky, trying to free itself from the confines of the park and bring hope to the creatures down below. I was in harmony with my world, exactly where I wanted to be, and this was the best hot dog ever.

The May Procession

The best thing about The May Procession was that we had to do it just once a year. But the agonizing preparations seemed to go on forever, as we were made to practice over and over. For several days prior, all of the elementary school students and teachers would empty out onto the sidewalk, in long lines, two by two, boys with boys, girls with girls, the nuns walking along side us with their clickers. We would slowly walk around the block, hands folded in prayer, fingers pointed upward to heaven, backs straight, eyes on our hands. The slightest deviation would be met with reprimand and perhaps punishment. When we got around the block we would file into the church and take our places in the pews, where we would practice our special songs for the occasion. The ceremony would culminate with the Queen of the May placing a crown of flowers on the head of statue of the Blessed Mother, at the side altar.

Being selected Queen of the May by the nuns was one of the highest honors a girl could receive, reserved for one of the older girls in the school. The Queen of the May would wear a white dress, like a wedding dress, with a long tail held up by younger girls. Back then, girls were only allowed through the gate and up to the altar when they married. But the girl selected as Queen of the May got to go up on the side altar and place the crown on Mary's head. As we all sang:

"Oh, Mary, we crown you with blossoms today

Queen of the angels

Queen of the May"

One year my sister, Ann, was selected. She was recovering from an operation and had a brace on her leg. She worried that it would squeak and be heard all through the church at the crucial moments of silence as she went to genuflect. She had Dad oil it.

Our aunt, Alberta, traveled from her home in another parish to see her niece on this golden day of her youth. Alberta sat up in the balcony and overheard women next to her whispering about the May Queen. "She's blind," said one, "and she makes all her own clothes."

Most years the May Procession had no such drama for us, just the boredom and tediousness of the proceedings. One year, one of my classmates devised a plan for getting out of it altogether. He said that, if you place ink blotters in your shoe they would draw the blood to your feet and you would pass out and be sent home. Once you took the blotters out you would be fine again. Blotters were like small pieces of sand paper that were used to blot out globs of ink that were left on paper from fountain pens. This was many years before ball point pens made blotters extinct. I was so tempted to try this, but I did not dare. I don't think my classmate did either.

Looking back on it now, it was probably quite lovely, all the children's voices raised in song, the pageantry, the Queen of the May crowning the mother of God. I so wish I could see it again, from the eyes of a wizened adult. At the time, it was just another hardship to be endured.

Aspirations

"...threeeee, twoooo, oneee!" I got the shot off as the clock ran down.

It hit the rim of the basket, rolled around it, then gracefully dropped through the net, just as the buzzer sounded to end the game. My shot broke the tie in the final nanosecond and we won the championship. I can't tell you how many times this happened to me while alone on the playground court. If I missed that shot the first time I just kept rewinding the clock and trying again until I made it. How I wished I could do that for real, in front of a huge, cheering crowd. I could have become a professional basketball player if it weren't for two things: Lack of talent and gravity.

I was just a young boy and I was already discarding future possibilities while my fantasy world kept expanding. When I was barely out of diapers I discovered Superman bending steel in his bare hands on TV. Back then there were news reports of kids jumping out of their second-story bedroom windows dressed as Superman, thinking they could actually fly. My parents worried about this. I seldom took off my superman pajamas. But I thought it best to try jumping off the sofa first. It didn't work. I could not fly. I would never be able to fly and I would never be able to jump high enough to dunk a basketball.

Playing second base for the Phillies was a possibility perhaps. I was a good fielder and a decent hitter. I also wanted to play saxophone in a rock and roll band. That would be cool. I convinced my parents to let me take lessons at school, but the nun in charge of the music department made me start with the clarinet. I learned to play it well enough that I got into the school orchestra. One Friday afternoon in the spring we had our final rehearsal before the annual Sunday concert. The last thing Sister Agnus told us was that everyone had to attend the concert. Anyone who did not show up for the concert without a very good reason would be thrown out of the music program.

Right after school that day I went to baseball practice. I was trying out for a little league team along with about a zillion other boys. I had made the first few cuts and was hanging in there with some very good players. The last thing the coach told us after practice that day was that the final cuts would take place at the next practice. That was on Sunday, about the same time as the school concert. He told us that anyone who missed the practice would be cut from the team.

I fretted about this all Friday night and all of Saturday. Would I rather be a rock and roll star or play second base for the Phillies? I was getting tired of the clarinet, and with Sister Agnus standing between me and the saxophone, music seemed like a difficult path. Was there some way I could keep both dreams alive? I thought that I could go to baseball practice and then show up at school with my thumb wrapped up in a big bandage. I would tell Sister Agnus that I broke my thumb on Saturday and could not play the clarinet. This seemed like a good idea, for about five minutes. Sister Agnus would probably want a note from a doctor or at least one from my mother. Lying to a nun would be a major offense and I would certainly be in big trouble both here and in my afterlife.

I decided to go to baseball practice. I was the last kid cut from the team. I lost out to the coach's son. I had to admit that he was good. I thought I was a better fielder, but he was a better hitter. I never even bothered showing up for the after-school music program again. So, in the course of one Sunday afternoon, two of my future career choices took a major setback.

Sewer Ball

A sense of dread overcame me as I watched the scene play out before me, like seeing an accident about to happen and knowing you can do nothing to prevent it. We were playing box ball on Van Kirk Street, our playground. Timmy skidded a hot grounder through the infield and the ball headed directly along the curb toward the sewer. It seemed to be propelled along by some internal force, driven, destined to reach the putrid water that ran beneath the ground. Kenny gave a desperate chase, but clearly it was too late.

The underworld was about to swallow a prized possession: the pimple ball, the bouncy sphere we used in most of our outdoor games. We used it for stick ball, wall ball, step ball and wire ball. When it broke and lost its air it usually cracked along the seam and we would cut it in half along that seam and get two half balls. Then all we needed was a broom handle and we had another game to play. One of the advantages of half ball was that it could be played with just two kids. The pitcher would stand in the middle of the street and float the half ball toward the curb where a kid with a stick would take a swing at it.

Hitting a half ball was a challenge, but when you connected just right it made a delightful sound and took off like a bullet. If it got past the pitcher it was a single. If it got past the curb on the other side of the street, it was a double. Down the alley to the back of the house with the clothes line was a triple. Four houses down was a home run, as was the roof tops on either side of the alley. We'd hate to see it land on the roof, but it sure did feel good to hit it up there. Most of us kept a stack of half balls in the house. Half ball was the most leisurely of ball games, requiring no running of the bases. Box ball, by contrast, required lots of kids to make two teams, and involved lots of running.

A pimple ball cost a whole dime, a mighty sum to us Philly kids in the fifties, barely a decade old. The basic way to come up with ten cents was to search the gutters and alleys for discarded soda bottles and take them to the corner store. The small ones were worth two cents and the big ones five cents. There were no cans or plastic containers back then and the deposit on the original purchased encouraged the return of the bottles for reuse. At the store, we had difficult consumer choices. For ten-cents we could get a comic book or two packs of baseball cards. The owners tried to steer us to the penny candies on display behind glass at the counter, but they preferred any exchange other that handing over the coins.

So, we were not about to let the sewer keep our ball. We had two options for retrieval. Both required lifting the heavy iron grate off the top of the sewer. We could then lower the scrawniest kid head first down with the two strongest kids holding onto his ankles, while the rest watched out for the cops or other adults who most likely would not approve of this procedure. Being a scrawny kid, I did not much care for this option. Even if my buddies were strong enough to lower me down I feared they just might panic and drop me if the cops came.

One time I was lowered down and just as I got the ball a long, a slimy, green hand came out from under the murky water, grabbed my wrist and tried to pull me under. I was caught in a tug-of-war between my friends and the horrible beast. Ok, that never actually happened, but it could have as far as I was concerned. I was still at an age of magical thinking. Ghost and goblins were all too real for me.

The second (preferred) option was to fish the ball out with a rake. That required locating a garden rake with hard teeth. Not a leaf rake with flimsy tines spread out at the end. That would never work. The problem was that we lived in a neighborhood of row houses with tiny, postage stamp lawns at best. There weren't gardens so there weren't garden rakes. So, we were amazed when Johnny ran off and came back with the rake we needed. He said that he borrowed it from his dad who wasn't home at the time, and his dad would kill him if we dropped the rake in the sewer.

I am pleased to report that this story has a happy ending. We fished out the ball and were soon back to the game. We decided, with some dispute, that the sewer ball was a ground-rule double and the runners took their bases accordingly. We picked a kid to stand in front of the sewer. He was too little to play with us but stood around whining and wanting to get in the game. We told him to be alert. If the ball came anywhere near him he must throw himself on top of it. We knew he couldn't catch it. We told him If it went down the sewer he would soon follow it, without anyone holding him by the ankles. The only down side was that we had to promise him a turn of hitting the ball with his fist like the rest of us. He did fine. He was just a little shrimp but he had potential.

Our enthusiasm for the game was considerably diminished by the delay, and soon the mothers began calling, as they did each day, from the back door:

"Jimmy, dinner's ready." "Tommy, supper time." So, off we trudged, valiant athletes, ready to rest up for another day of competition on the street.

Age of Wonder

I vividly remember the first time I saw one. It was in the alley behind my house on Loretto Avenue in the Oxford Circle area of Philadelphia. It was the late 1950's and I was about eleven years old. My buddy, Johnny, was holding a small, plastic thing in his hand. It was thin and rectangular, and it was making noise. It sounded like the static of a radio trying to find a station. It was a radio trying to find a station. But how could that be? A radio required tubes and a big box to hold them in.

Johnny explained that this was a transistor radio, running on a little battery and requiring no tubes. If you found just the right spot in the alley, and turned the little tuning wheel just right, you could pull in radio stations. He opened it up to show me the strange little, intricately wired board inside. How could such a small, cheap looking thing produce such wonder?

The application of this marvelous breakthrough in technology was immediately apparent. Back then the major-league baseball World Series was played out during the day, when we were in school. We could put this device in our pocket, plug in the long wire with the ear piece on the end that came with it, run the wire up under our shirt, and place the end in our ear. While pretending to listen attentively to our teacher, we could actually be listening to the World Series. But we would have to be very careful. I shuddered to think what would happen if I got caught.

But I'm certain I would have actually tried this if the Philadelphia Phillies had ever gotten to the Series when I was young. But they were a sad team back then. It wasn't worth the risk to listen to the despicable Yankees win yet another Series. Still, I delighted in thinking that some boy in our class may be listening to baseball as I was listening to my teacher drone on about the Civil War, or the proper use of adverbs. So perhaps I should be grateful that the Phillies were so bad back then. If they had been in the Series I would have tried that trick with the radio. I probably would have been caught and punished severely and that may have started me on a life of crime. One never knows.

Shortly after I discovered the transistor radio I had another experience with the wonder of technology, also related to baseball. I was watching a Phillies game on the TV (black and white, of course) when the announcer urged us to stay tuned for something very special in the next inning. I certainly needed this encouragement because the home team was about to complete another humiliating loss. I did stay tuned, and boy was it worth it. The very next inning they were able to show a replay of a play from the previous inning! How could they do that? How could they develop the film so fast? A few years later my buddy, Kenny, got something called a tape recorder, and we would often gather in his bedroom to produce our own radio shows. Technology was moving along at a marvelously fast pace.

Now technology moves along at such a fast pace that I can't keep up. I resist every new advance, relenting only when the benefits outweigh my resistance and the latest thing has become a necessary thing in our culture. I would have grumbled about the invention of the printing press if I had been alive back then. Think of all the poor scribes it put out of work. I may have relented to it only when it produced the first baseball book.

Perhaps the true tests of any new advance in technology should be how it would help the Philadelphia Phillies win a World Series.

The Delpark Club

Every once in a while, on a Sunday morning, Dad would get the urge to take his boys to mass at his old parish, St. Stephens. My brothers and I would eagerly hop in the car, and off we'd go. The church was in a section of the city that had seen better days. On the drive, Dad would reminisce, regaling us with wild tales of his youth on the mean streets of Philadelphia, where ragged boys roamed, engaging in various kinds of games and mischief. I was captivated as I tried to imagine him as a boy.

When we got to the church we would park and climb the steps, but sometimes Dad would realize that we had arrived too late. The mass had already begun, and we had missed the first of the three essential parts of the mass required to meet our Sunday obligation. Seemingly dejected, Dad would decide that, since we had come all this way, we should go to the Delpark Club.

The club was a sports association and Dad was a founding member. Back when he was single, he played minor league baseball and was respected for his skill covering the center of the infield, playing second base. He and his ball buddies decided to form their own club. The first priority of such clubs was to get a liquor license and open a bar. The bar was for members only, which allowed it to be open on Sundays. The Philly "blue laws" prohibited the serving of alcohol by commercial establishments. So, there we went. We were delighted.

As we entered the club we were overwhelmed by the ambiance. The aroma of the night before hung in the air like the incense of benediction. Clearly much had happened here. A few old guys sat at the bar. Dad ushered us to a booth directly below the life-size photo of the sacred trinity of baseball: Babe Ruth, Lou Gehrig and Jimmy Fox. Communion was served: stale pretzels and flat ginger ale in whiskey-soaked glasses. We were as close to Heaven as possible on Earth.

Inevitably, a few of Dad's old buddies would stop by to chew the fat, catching up and sharing memories. Sometimes I felt I could sit there forever, but the time would come when we had to go home. On the way, Dad would say how sad it was that we missed the mass, then told us that there was no need to tell this to Mom. No such thought had ever entered our minds. We had missed the mass, but I had no doubt that we had fulfilled our Sunday obligation. I can think of no other experience as sacred as visiting the Delpark Club on a Sunday morning.

Soda Jerk

I worked at Melrose Pharmacy when I was in high school (early '60s). The drug store was on the corner of Oxford and Loretto, just a block away from the Oxford Circle in Northeast Philly. I look back on the experience now as, perhaps, the best job I ever had. The commute was half a block on foot. I didn't even have to cross a street. The work schedule and pay met my needs perfectly. I could swap times with my coworkers and I got paid each Friday, in cash, bills tucked inside a brown pay envelop. The money was just enough to cover my expenses, which were not much since Mom and Dad paid the bills. Being able to cover movies, dates, and toiletries gave me a sense of independence.

Merv Melrose was a good boss and a very nice man. He took a real interest in his employees and in our families. I worked the soda fountain and later as a clerk back in the pharmacy. On my first day on the job he told me I could eat all the ice cream and drink all the soda I wanted. I knew that he knew I would soon get sick of soda and ice cream, but I took him up on the offer anyway. It was sort of a rite of passage, something I just had to endure to become one of the boys. Yes, it was strictly a male cadre back then.

George Louie, who owned the Chinese laundry across the street, would often stop in and chat with Merv and, on a slow night, he would stay late. They would get into long, interesting discussions back in the pharmacy. I often caught bits of it from my perch at the fountain, enough to form the opinion that these were two smart and inquisitive men who enjoyed each other's company. They talked about the neighborhood, their lives and current event. They exchanged ideas and opinions. They seemed to have a lot in common, the Jewish pharmacist and the Chinese laundryman.

As was common at the time, both men lived at their businesses, Merv above his and George in a big house behind the laundry. Both were married and had kids at home. Merv had two young boys, George had gazillion boys and girls, or so it seemed. Merv also provided me with advice about life, always unsolicited but usually on the mark. We were not called "soda jerks" back then. I didn't learn of that term until many years later, but when I did, I took it on with pride.

Merv was the first one consulted by Mom and several others in the neighborhood when there was a health issue. He listened, asked questions and came up with good advice, often helping to avoid the cost of a doctor's visit.

One day Merv told me he was thinking of taking out the soda fountain. I was shocked. The soda fountain was a traditional gathering place in the neighborhood, much like the bars and places of worship, but open to all. You didn't need to be over 21 or have any particular religious beliefs. How could he possibly be thinking such heresy?

That was exactly the problem, he explained. Just about anyone could come and sit for long periods of time sipping a ten-cent soda or a free seltzer water. It was a waste of valuable retail space. He could fill all that space with products that customers would want and buy and leave so more customers could come and buy and leave. I told him that this would be a very unpopular change. He said that everyone would get over it in time.

He did make the change and it was very unpopular. Customers did get over it, and I went from being a soda jerk to being a pharmacy clerk. This was a lateral move with the same pay. I didn't like it at first, but I too, got over it. That soda fountain is long gone now, and so are many of the people who frequented it, including Merv Melrose and George Louie. Somewhere a drug store with a soda fountain may still exist, but for the most part, time and progress have left them behind.

Beer Decision

To drink or not to drink

The beer distributor on the corner of Oxford and Loretto may be the longest continually operated business in the Oxford Circle section of Philly. The pharmacy, laundry and car dealership that once shared the intersection are long gone. This is not surprising considering the staying power of beer. With roots in antiquity, the beverage was probably consumed at the dawn of civilization, or perhaps at the more respectable lunch hour that day.

A few years ago, I went back there with my sister, Kathy. Over fifty years had passed since the last time I stood on that corner and this was the first time I was old enough to enter the establishment. Back in the day (circa1950's) it wasn't necessary to enter the building to experience the essence of the place. It spilled out all over the sidewalk and street, bustling with busy men loading and unloading trucks, the pavement stacked with cases of bottles and metal kegs. The doors were always wide open and the proprietor was boisterous and jovial. In December, he blared loud Christmas music from speakers mounted on the roof. It was ear-numbing, even at a reasonable distance, partially absorbed by the row of mostly Jewish owned homes on that block of Oxford Avenue, testing the limits of religious tolerance.

Beer was delivered to our house on foot. I believe delivery was free within a certain limited radius, as far as was reasonable for a man to carry a case of bottles on his shoulder. We were well within this parameter. It was a short walk across Oxford Avenue and half way down the alley behind the short row of houses facing Loretto. The man would climb the back stairs, drop the new case on the small landing outside the kitchen door and take the case of empties back.

The choices were very limited. A person could get lagers from Milwaukee or Philly area lagers (Schmidt, Ortlieb, Yuengling or Ballantine.) Visitors from the old world were rightly appalled. They all tasted very much the same. The top of the line was Miller High Life, marketed pretentiously as "the champagne of bottled beers." In order to punctuate this elitist claim, it came in clear bottles, which I later learned is a very bad idea, light being the enemy of beer and vampires. But the marketing allowed it to be sold at a premium price, far more expensive than the others. Dad, a man of modest means, always went for whatever was the cheapest.

One day Dad opened the back door to find a case of Miller's High Life, sparkling like gold. He quickly concluded that this was a gift from a friend or relative and set about chilling it. Mom had a different take on this. She was certain it was a mistaken delivery, and one we could not afford. There were bills to pay and kids to feed. This was far too extravagant an indulgence.

Beer has been a topic of interest for poets, sages and philosophers for eons. A.E. Houseman wrote: "Malt does more than Milton can to justify God's ways to man". Benjamin Franklin is attributed with saying beer is proof that God loves us and wants us to be happy. He probably didn't actually say that, but he did enjoy his drink. Neither of these gentlemen lived in our neighborhood at the time, but if they had and were asked for an opinion, I think they would have sided with Dad and graciously helped him consume the brew. But the three men together would not be a match for Mom when she got her dander up. She was usually acquiescent to Dad's wishes, as was customary for wives at the time. But there were times when her German backbone proved resistant to Dad's Irish charms. This was one of those times. She put her foot down and, sure enough, this was a delivery mistake.

Dad had to return the beer and settle for his every day swill.

On our recent visit my sister and I found the current proprietors, man and woman, settled down for lunch, eating out of bowls with chopsticks in a little office behind security glass. The man quickly rose and helped us, politely and efficiently, as we picked from the mind-numbing choices and varieties. When my sister mentioned our history with the neighborhood and the establishment he had no reaction. Most likely, he was impatient to get back to his meal.

Sometimes it is the little things that can change the course of human history. I've heard it said, for example, that Luther's constipation caused the reformation. I wonder what would have happened if Dad had consumed that case of Miller's. Would we have been unable to pay the bills and been thrown out on the street? Would it have tipped the balance of power in my parent's relationship and destroyed their marital bond? Probably not, but you never know for sure. Sometimes things just work out for the best.

Ronan

"Take your hands out of your pockets. There's no reason you should have any more fun than the rest of us." These words burst from the month of Mr. Ronan, our Freshman English teacher.

They were directed at Jimmy Hughes, the slight 14-year-old picked to read the part of Juliet. We were studying Shakeshit, the common name for the Bard amongst my peers. Jimmy, standing now in the front of the room, was considerably less than thrilled at the opportunity, but ours was an all-boys Catholic high school. Some boy must read the part if we were going to do this, which none of us wanted to do in the first place. But now the exercise was taking on the excitement of ridicule and the air in the room was charged with the powerful energy released by a bunch of hormonally overcharged boys.

The nuns in grade school had warned us repeatedly when we were misbehaving: "Just wait till you get into high school." We took this to mean that we, subjected to the rule of men, would undergo punishment much worse than what the nuns could deliver with their rulers, clickers and yardsticks. This turned out to be true, but we had never been warned that we may also be subject to provocative adult humor

109

such as Mr. Ronan had just provided us. His words were shocking and delightful and we responded with a roar of laughter.

Mr. Ronan was a big, beefy man with a slightly effeminate manner. Normally this would provide fodder for my classmates, on the ready to insult anyone with any sign of weakness, real or imagined. But not Mr. Ronan. He had a justly earned reputation for being someone students didn't want to mess with. His vengeance was legendary and he seemed constantly on the alert for any opportunity to release his pent-up aggression. He looked forward each year to the annual student vs faculty "touch" football game. Lacking any protective equipment, this form of the sport commonly played in streets and alleys, was intended to simulate tackle football in every way eccept for the clashing of bodies. Blocking was prohibited and "tackles" were made simply by placing two hands on the runner. Mr. Ronan interpreted the rules rather loosely, and each year targeted students (i.e. tough guys and wise guys) would end up bruised and beaten. A certain amount of levity was permitted in his class if and when he was in the mood, but we quickly had to learn the limits.

The school brought in kids from surrounding working-class neighborhoods assigned by the dioceses based on some map of territories set up like feudal kingdoms. Our school was overcrowded and populated by the sons of Irish, German and Polish families with strong ethnic identities. It was sometimes called "Animal Farm." I was trying to find my place in this menagerie and my best opportunity seemed to be taking on the role of class clown. In the lunchroom, I could attract a crowd by doing satirical imitations of teachers. In class I could get a laugh by providing clever verbal zingers. These had to be timed and phrased carefully to press but not exceed the limits imposed by various teachers.

Jimmy's hands had been deep in the pockets of his trousers, but I never would have thought to connect that to self-stimulation of the genitals. To hear a teacher do so was astounding. Mr. Ronan was also opening the door for verbal play and I so wanted to join in that. The problem was that the other actors had not yet been picked and I didn't want to do anything to draw attention. I was, in fact, trying to hide myself behind the boy sitting in front of me. But Joey Clemente was about as little as I was. I was leaning over, almost resting my head on the desk, wishing I were sitting behind Larry Gronkowski, a lineman on the football team, who had not only a lot of bulk but shoulders near as wide as my height. But we were made to sit alphabetically so that could never happen.

Somehow, I managed to escape being picked that day, but I was not always so fortunate. Humiliation was part of our educational experience back in 1961. Perhaps it still is so today. It is as inevitable in life as taxes and death. It can happen without effort, but I can't imagine anyone better at inflicting it than Mr. Ronan.

Towards the end of the year Mr. Ronan called Jimmy Hughes and me up to the front of the room and made us face the class. He told the class to take a good look at us. He said he had been a teacher for many years and could always tell. He said that Jimmy and I would never make it to graduation. I was shocked. I hadn't even been doing anything wrong at the time. My grades weren't great but they weren't terrible either. Jimmy was gone by the end of the year. I took it as a challenge. I don't recall making any real changes after that, but his words were constantly perched in my mind. I stuck it out and graduated from the school. I can't say for sure but maybe I would not have made it if it were not for Mr. Ronan.

Juno

I felt awkward, very awkward. I was standing alone in a dimly lit gymnasium, surrounded by other kids like me, attempting to shed off our adolescents and spread our wings, at the school dance. My buddies had already scattered out, checking out the girls while pretending not to notice them. Early on we just hung out together, the boys on one side the girls on the other. But when we began to mix it got more complicated.

I had four sisters so I knew what girls were like, how they talked and occupied their time. But that didn't seem to help me much at the moment. It also didn't help that I attended an all-boys Catholic high school, providing me with no opportunity to talk to girls who were not my sisters. I knew I had to do like my buddies, pick a girl and ask her to dance. It would have to be a slow dance. A fast dance would be much too embarrassing. If she accepted my invitation we would shuffle around the dance floor for a few minutes and then that part would be over. But that part would involve feeling her breast against my chest, which would most likely arouse me to such an extent that I would be totally embarrassed. Then what should I do?

Assuming I got through that, what should I do next? I watched the older boys intently for an answer. They asked the girl her name and then asked where she was from. Once she identified her neighborhood, the next phase of the mating ritual would begin. It was a game I call "Juno."

The boy would say where he was from and then they would try to find some connection with each other through a family member, friend or acquaintance who lived in the neighborhood of the other. The boy might begin by asking, "Juno my cousin Kenny Sasser? He lives near you."

On the first try, the answer was usually "No." But, if the girl was even remotely interested in you she would reply: "Juno Betty McGonagall? We were best friends in grade school. She lives just around the corner from you."

This could go on and on painfully, but the desire to find some connection was a sign of willingness to endure in hopes of establishing some connection that might begin a meaningful relationship.

"Juno Jonny Burgess?"

"Juno Alice Simpkins?"

"Juno Tony Geraldo?"

"Juno Marge Flesher?"

The longer you struggled at this stage the more gratifying the relationship might be once you found somebody, a second cousin once removed perhaps, who you actually both knew. Sometimes it was a bit of a stretch, when pretending to know of someone was close enough.

Could I get through that? The night was getting late. It was now or never. I spotted a girl sitting alone across the room. She had long blond hair and a nice smile. A sweet song started to play:

"When I want you, in my arms

When I want you, and all your charms,

Whenever I want you all I have to do is dream."

I shuffled my feet, crossed the room and popped the question.

Secret Sears Santa

When I was a lad, back in the 60's, I worked for a while at the Sears store on the Roosevelt Boulevard in Northeast Philly. I started off part-time while I was in high school and then worked a year full-time while I went to LaSalle College at night. The job helped me save enough money so I could, with the help of a student loan, go to school full-time the following year. My job was in catalogue pick-up, on the second floor of what was then a new, modern facility. I had a great boss, Mr. Pomeroy, the manager of the department. Most of my co-workers were young folks like me, in similar circumstances, and Mr. Pomeroy was a kind, fatherly figure.

During the Christmas season things got rather hectic. Catalogue sales was a big business back then, in a world before Amazon. I doubt if there was a single household that did not receive the annual Christmas catalogue in the mail, more than five inches thick and full of coveted merchandise. Orders were usually phoned in and picked up a few days later. When customers came to the pick-up counter one of us would pull the order ticket and clip it overhead on a carousel line that would take it back behind the wall to the retail warehouse. There one of us would pull the order off the clip, hustle to the matching bin, pull the package, clip on the ticket and place the order on a conveyor belt. It would travel up high and come down a chute to the pick-up desk. There one of us would get the package, call out the name and complete the purchase.

Purchases were mostly cash, and we had to have all the bills stacked up neatly and in perfect order when we walked over to the cashier, a stern woman who wore rhinestone glasses attached with a silver chain around her neck. If a single bill was facing the wrong way, or had a crimp in a corner, she would send us away until we got it straight. This system was invented, I was told, by a young worker like me.

In was a fine system most of the time, but at Christmas it was pressed to the limit and we just could not always keep up. The tickets would go around and around on the carousel, a sure sign that the lads in the back were falling behind. The packages would back up on the chute and conveyor belt. Customers packed the room and were not happy when their order was not ready, misplaced or just wrong. The woman who ordered shoes and got two left footed shoes was not happy. The man who ordered paint and got the wrong color looked calm at first. Then he opened the lid, dumped the gallon of paint upside down on the counter and walked away.

Then one day it happened. I got to the store before it opened, as usual. I was let in the employee's entrance and got on the escalator. There, waiting for me at the top of the escalator was a beautiful woman, dressed in a most revealing, sheer red negligee. She wore a matching red Santa hat. There was no one else around, just the two of us. She stood there, posed so provocatively. She was a mannequin, of course, but that didn't stop me from blushing. I had a severe blushing problem back then and was working to overcome it as diligently as I fought the pimples on my face. She was more mature than the girls I knew, yet she seemed to be there for me, natural and enticing.

I was aroused and thought about her all that shift. I fantasized about her at night in ways I would surely have to tell in confession as "impure thoughts." I'd try to pick a priest who did not ask questions. I didn't what to have to explain that a mannequin was the source of my lust. I would try so hard not to sin in this way again, but I would surely fail. She was there for me each day and I looked forward to our brief encounters. I could tell no one. I had never met anyone like her before. There were the underwear models in the Sears catalogue. They were attractive and often less covered that my new friend, but they were just pictures. This woman was life-size and looked so real. I wanted to touch her skin, to talk to her, to embrace her. I never told anyone about this before and perhaps I should not now. I had forgotten about it until just recently when the memory came back to me in vivid color, like visions of sugar plums.

The Sears store has now been demolished and I have no idea what happened to her. I hope she aged gracefully. Perhaps she went on to model maternity clothing and then granny panties before retiring from Sears with a nice pension and the ten percent discount.

I'd like to tell her how much she meant to me and wish her a Merry Christmas.

Off to the Races

A new race track was opening in Northeast Philly, just up the boulevard from our house. My sisters, Ann and Charlotte, were going and they offered to take me. No one under twenty-one years of age was allowed in, and I was about nineteen at the time. I looked like I was closer to fifteen. But my sisters encouraged me to give it a try. Some of their friends were going. I could hide in the middle of their group. One of them would buy all the tickets, so I would not have to show my face at the ticket counter. If I didn't get in I could drive their car home and they would have their friends drop them off at home after the races.

The track was for Trotters and Pacers, with each horse pulling a two-wheeled cart called a sulky, occupied by a driver. This was all new to me. I had no interest in horse racing of any kind, but this seemed like a fun night out. Low and behold, our plan worked. I got in and we were soon seated and enjoying the spectacle. Then the time came when we were supposed to place our bets. I have never much enjoyed gambling of any sort. I played penny-poker with friends from time to time and enjoyed it but got little thrill from winning. And I don't like losing my hard-earned money.

So, I did not bet on the first few races. I enjoyed just sitting there and watching. But I concluded that the night would not be complete unless I placed a bet. I randomly picked out a horse from the lineup and decided to place a two-dollar bet, the lowest amount permitted. I gave my sisters the money. I did not want to show my face at the betting window where I would most likely be flagged and thrown out for being too young.

That race now took on new importance for me and I was excited as the race began. With this kind of racing the sulkies and horses line up behind a pace car, an actual automobile with long wings on the back. The car starts off and the horses follow. The car goes faster, then folds up its wings and drives out of the way. Just as the wings began to fold, my horse stopped, turned around and went running off in the opposite direction. The driver worked hard to get it turned back around. Then he ran it hard, actually catching up to the back of the pack. But by this time my horse had just spent too much energy. I was out two bucks, but I had a good story to tell.

Many years later, after I moved to Indiana, friends invited us to go to Keenland, a thoroughbred horse track in Kentucky for an event similar to the Kentucky Derby. It had all the pageantry on a smaller scale. We were having great fun enjoying the food, drink and pleasant ambience. Then I decided to place a bet. It was my first since that fateful day in Philly. I picked a horse with a name I liked, and again placed the minimum bet. Once again, I was excited when the horses shot out of the gate. I had a hard time picking my horse out from the pack, but when I did I was delighted to see it running close to the front on the backstretch. There was just one problem. There was no jockey on its back. Somewhere on the far side of the track where I could not see, the two had gotten separated.

My horse did not finish first. If it had I would have argued that I won the bet. What difference did it make that it had no jokey? I bet on the horse not the rider. I had to break the jinx, so I did bet on other races that day. I won a few and lost a few. I have not bet on a horse since then. But if you would like my advice on picking a winner just let me know.

The Wild Kids and the School Bus

For a year of my life I was a substitute school bus driver in Bucks County, Pennsylvania. This was a rural area though it is much less so today. Near here George Washington crossed the Delaware one cold winter night to surprise and defeat the Hessians, which helped turn the tide of our revolutionary war. Some days it was easy for me to relate to such an experience.

I'd rise up before the sun on a bitter cold winter morn and face a day of dangers and threats. A labyrinth of roads covered the rolling countryside. Many were narrow and sometimes covered with ice or snow. My mission was clear. I was to pick up sleepy eyed kids and get them safely to their respective schools. At the end of the school day I was to pick kids up at various schools and get them safely home. This sounded so simple.

I passed the driver training and got my license, learning to tame the yellow behemoth – the great yellow beast with flashing eyes that ate the children in the morning and spit them out in the afternoon. I thought I was ready for the next battle. I was at a disadvantage as a substitute since I had no knowledge of the routes. I would be called, sometime the night before, and asked if I could take over for Ernie who's having gallbladder problems again or Burt who pulled his back. I'd pick up the bus and the paper with the route, which I could not see in the dark (paper or route). I'd find my way to the first stop. I'd hand the paper to the first sleepy child up the bus steps, with instructions to get me to the next stop. I continue this approach throughout the trip, drafting more kids to help find the way. Amazingly, the system worked. I only had one complaint of a missed stop my entire year of service. But going home was a much different challenge.

There is often little resemblance between morning kids and afternoon kids, especially when they have been put through the brain grinder of the US educational system. Afternoon kids are wired and squirmy and tired of being made to be good. They are packed together in the great bus beast, pushing and shoving each other off and on at the various schools and lanes. Their parting rituals can be particularly eventful.

Most notorious of the subgroups was the junior high bunch. Ranging in age from 11 to 14, these were the kids in between child and teenager. They also seemed at times to be in between awareness and unawareness, reality and fantasy, darkness and light. This group featured a wide range of sizes and unpredictable, sudden and drastic changes in behavior and attitude.

My strategy for the home trip was simple and effective. I took advantage of the fact that, most of all, these kids wanted to get home. If my verbal warnings did not work I would simply pull the bus off to the side of the road and refuse to move till they settled down.

One Friday afternoon I found myself near the end of a route with a riotous gaggle of the in-between kids. After a full week of school, they were letting loose. They were wild and loud and seemingly out of control. My increasingly intense verbal reprimands had no effect. I saw my opportunity as I turned onto a highway with plenty of room on the shoulder. I pull the bus over and stood to face them and declare my stubborn intent. To my horror they all stood and headed towards me in a mass. Were they planning to overthrow me? Were they really capable of such treason? I stared in disbelief, but saw no anger in their eyes. Then I heard one say goodbye. They stopped in front of me waiting for me to get out of the way and open the door. They all lived in the housing development directly across the road. This was the exact spot of their bus stop. When I realized this, I acted as if I knew it all along. I was just getting up to stretch my legs. I sat back down, opened the door and let them pass. The last little boy off the bus turned and asked me why I stopped so far off the road. I simply waved goodbye.

Some lessons cannot be learned in school. Sometimes, just when you think you have everything figured out, fate will twist you about. Sometimes you land on your feet and other times on your head. Call it luck or fate or fortune or a blessing. Life offers ample opportunity for humiliation, and some for covering your tracks.

Missing Pieces

I got off the Metro bus and walked a few blocks to my home in North Baltimore. It was early spring in 1968. I was returning from a workout at the downtown YMCA. I was a VISTA Volunteer, a two-year commitment often referred to as the domestic Peace Corps. I was renting a row house with two other white VISTA workers in a poor, black neighborhood and working out of a nearby settlement house providing community services.

When I walked in the door I realized that the only one there was Leroy, a boy from the neighborhood. He was watching TV. This was not unusual. Kids often hung out at our place, and they were never a problem. They treated our place well and we never felt a need to protect our meager belongings. Leroy was a bright and friendly kid, about eleven years old. He had a good sense of humor and a ready smile.

I was there for just a few moments when the program on the TV was interrupted for a special message. The Reverend Martin Luther King, Jr. had just been assassinated. The shock of this announcement was immediately followed by another. Leroy looked at me and asked, "Who's Martin Luther King?"

That's about all the pieces I can find that bring back episodes from the tumultuous period of the 1960's and 70's, a time when I graduated from high school and came of age, got through college, entered the world of adult work, got married and had a kid. It was a time of great upheaval in the nation and the world, which bled into my personal life in so many ways.

I do recall much of that time, but what I am experiencing with this puzzle is more like reliving than recalling. Reliving in compressed time. I have most of the edge pieces connected now, but I'm still missing a few. I can clearly see that this must be a thousand - piece puzzle. I am making progress on the interior and can see that it is definitely the image of me depicted on the top of the box. I can also see that I do not have nearly enough pieces left to complete it. I will have to go back up to the attic and search for more. If I find pieces that bring back this period of my past I know it will be very difficult to relive. Those missing pieces would make the connection, explaining how I ended up in that room with Leroy, in front of that TV at that moment.

Missing is the story of how I met my wife, who somehow still manages to put up with me after so many years. Missing is the story of what happened to my religious beliefs. A nun once told me that the worst possible of all beings were fallen-away Catholics. They were even worse than heathens, who never saw the light. Fallen-away Catholics had seen the light and turned their backs to it. I was more of a run-away Catholic than a fallen away one. My spiritual voyage took many a turn. The distance from the Catholic Church helped me to see it more objectively, and appreciate the good it did for me, providing me with a decent education and a moral path to be followed, difficult as that might be at times, for me and for the Church itself.

Missing also are all of the most embarrassing moments of my life, all the really dumb and insensitive things I have done over the years. I hope I never find those pieces.

Two nights after that moment with Leroy, I got a frantic and urgent call from my mother. She just heard on the news that race riots broke out in Baltimore. Was I alright? I assured her I was and that there was no rioting going on in my neighborhood. I hung up the phone and went upstairs to my bedroom. I looked out the window to the east. The horizon was ablaze with fire and smoke. Sirens and crashing sounds filled the air. I would soon be in the middle of it all.

Every time I think back to that period I have more questions than answers. I wonder about how and why it all happened. I wonder about how it shaped me, and how it shaped Leroy. I remember him as a fine lad and I hope he grew to be a fine man, that he still has that sweet smile, and that he managed to retain his sense of humor. I hope that, from an early age, the children in my old Baltimore neighborhood are now taught about the civil rights movement and learn the names of those men and women who shaped it.

On the trail

I was sitting next to Jack who had just taken his turn behind the wheel of his VW Microbus. We were on our way to the southern end of the Appalachian Trail in Georgia for our long awaited two-week backpacking adventure. We were near the end of a long drive from Pennsylvania, but still had a far piece to go. We were now in the mountains and the narrow winding road slowed our progress considerably. I commented to Jack that it seemed like we were getting unbelievably good gas mileage. It was many miles since our last refill and the needle on the gauge indicated that the tank was almost have full. Jack reached over and tapped the gauge and the needle dropped below empty. It had been stuck.

It was almost like this trip was cursed from the beginning. We had difficulty coordinating our schedules to get the time off work, then Jack came down with the flu a few days before our planned departure. This set us back a few weeks. It was March and we decided to do the southern end because it would be more like spring there, or so we hoped. As it turned out, the area was being hit by a major ice storm. But we were determined to make this happen.

If we could just get to the park at the southern end we could camp there for a day or two until the weather improved. But could we get there? There were no signs of civilization around us and we hadn't seen anything but woods for several miles now. We were heading from remote to more remote with each twisting turn. What was the likelihood of us finding a gas station? At least we were going downhill. Perhaps we could coast into the park on an empty tank. A quick look at the map put that idea to rest. The distance was too great and it was not all downhill. There were places where we found ourselves climbing again.

Lo and behold, like an oasis in a desert, a gas station appeared. It was an old, dilapidated wreak of a place, but it had a pump and a sign saying it was open. The proprietor looked like he belonged in this setting, like a hillbilly out of central casting. He was taciturn but helpful enough. We got a tank full of the precious petrol and were soon on our way again. Then, just minutes from the park, Jack notice that the minibus was acting peculiar. It was pulling and grinding. We limped into the park.

There a friendly ranger told us that a heated cabin with a bath was available for the next few days. We booked it for the night. The storm was setting in now but we didn't want to spend too much time in a cabin. That was not what we drove all this way for. Hopefully the weather would improve. The ranger could not confirm that. He looked doubtful. We spent two nights in the cabin as the icy rain continued. Jack located a garage that sent a guy to tow his microbus. It had a broken axle. It would take several days to get and install a new one. The rain stopped, so we decided to pack up and push off on the trail. Jack said there was no use to wait on the microbus. According to our AT Guide Book there were a few places we would be hiking where we might be able to get to a phone to call the garage. We got the latest forecast from the ranger. It called for high winds and maybe snow, but no rain. That was as good as it was going to get. We could handle that.

We were experienced with winter backpacking on the AT and were well prepared. For several years, on the first really miserable day of late fall or early winter, we would get a call from our friend Charlie. When we answered the phone, Charlie would say "It is time!" We knew what this meant. It was a challenge. Several of us would get together to hike a section of the trail for a few days. We hiked in all kinds of difficult weather. Rain was the worst. Once you and all your gear got wet it would be miserable and very cold. We could just brush off snow and get a fire going when we camped. Not so with rain. We had endured and actually enjoyed these trips, but we had never been on the AT or any trail as long as Jack and I planned to this time.

So, we pushed off for the approach trail. We found the spot on the map, but it could not be correct. The guide book said it would be a gradual incline to the connection with the AT. The narrow path we were looking at went straight up. But this was the connection trail. This was our first indication, often confirmed along the way, that the guide book seriously understated the degree of difficult on many sections. We made the climb, at times grabbing on to whatever roots or limbs we could reach to pull ourselves up. Our backpacks were already feeling heavy.

We made the connection to the AT and were slowly on our way. The wind was howling and there was enough of a snow to make it hard to see. There were many limbs down from the storm that we had to go over, under or around. We got to one huge tree that had fallen across the trail. We could not go over or under it. We had to go around it. But which way? We couldn't see the ends of it in either direction. I thought going to the right looked best. Jack did not agree. So, we went in opposite directions, trying to find our way around the fallen behemoth. We soon lost sight of each other but tried to keep in verbal contact. That soon became impossible as the howling wind obliterated all other sound. When I made my way around the crown of the fallen tree I had trouble finding my way back to the trail. I had to work my way through think brush and got a bit disorientated. I wasn't sure if I was heading in the right direction.

It took a while, but I did get back on the trail and Jack did also. We agreed that, if we encountered another such obstacle, we would stay together. The rest of the day went okay but, after the difficult start, we didn't make near as much progress as we planned. Before nightfall we decided to pitch our tent in a gap between two peaks, thinking we would be protected from the wind there. That was not the case. As we soon realized, the gap was where the wind went through. It was like being in a wind tunnel. The thin fabric of the tent flapped rapidly most of the night. Jack read aloud from "The Hobbit" by the light of our little battery-operated lantern. We somehow managed to fall asleep.

We awoke sometime before dawn to a loud, blood-curdling, screeching somewhere on the peak above us. My first thought was it sounded like a woman being torture. Was this a crazed hillbilly domestic dispute? No, this was a beast that was descending the peak and headed directly for us. The sound got closer and closer. Clearly, this beast from hell was making its way down from the mountain and towards us. It seemed to get very close and then it suddenly and completely stopped as the sun slowly lit the sky.

Later that day we met two guys who were aspiring through-hikers, attempting to complete the entire 2,186 miles in one trip, starting at the southern end and hoping to make it all the way to northern end, finishing with a climb up Mount Katahdin in Maine before the worst of winter. One of them told us that the sounds we heard during the night were that of a Bobcat. We had no idea that such a little creature could make such a loud and horrible noise. The other guy was a nineteen-year old who had recently recovered from having both of his knees replaced.

We hiked along with them for a few days, but then they just out-paced us. We were getting into our own daily rhythm and enjoying the fantastic vistas and the beauty of the earth beneath our feet. It remained cold enough for us to keep on our down coats. Then one night I got the flu. We were in a shelter and I awoke in the middle of the night feeling odd, feverish and a bit delirious. I had a sudden need to relieve my bowels. I climbed out of my sleeping back and made my way a short distance into the brush, where I squatted.

Then I heard the sound of automatic gun fire and a rustling of the brush around me. Or was I just imaging that? Then I remember reading in the guide book that this was an area where the army often practiced maneuvers. We hadn't heard any such sounds as we hiked, but that had to be the explanation. I was relieved, in more ways than one. I got back to my sleeping bag, crawled in and spent the remainder of the night in a weird, almost out-of-body state of mind.

When the light came I sat serenely watching the snow gently fall on us and told Jack that I could not go on. I was sick, very sick. I could hardly move. We came up with a plan. Late the previous afternoon, just after we set up at the sheltered we were visited by three young guys carrying nothing but a big jug of wine and a pocket full of joints. One of them explained that he brought his two friends up to show them the picnic table his grandfather had made many years ago. We noticed how unusual it was when we arrived. He said that it was made from a large tree and the sawed pieces had to be carried up to the sheltered and then assembled. No trees of that size grew up on this rocky peak. They told us they just drove up on a whim as far as they could and hiked the rest of the way. They shared their wine with us and hiked back down to sleep in their vehicle, a VW Microbus.

If we could hike down and catch them before they drove away, he could ask them to drive us down to the nearest town. We could get a motel room and Jack could call to check on his vehicle repair. This worked out just as we hoped. We were a sorry sight for the women at the motel desk. We were very dirty and I was very sick. For a moment I thought she might refuse to give us a room. But she gave us one. I suspect that this was not her first encounter with AT refuges. I had a most delightful hot bath, crawled naked between to clean sheets and slept, off and on, through the day and the night. Jack's VW was fixed and he was able to hitch-hike to get it. I was feeling better in the morning. I could have used another day in bed, but I didn't want to give up another day we could be spending on the trail.

We drove to an approach trail and were back on our way. My pace was slow that day, but by the next I was getting back to normal. Fortunately, the bug that was going around was a 24-hour type flu. We finished up our days on the trail without further incident. The weather got better and better. We didn't make near the distance we had originally planned, but we were pleased with what we did accomplish considering the problems we had to deal with. Terry hitch-hiked back and got his VW as I waited with the packs. The drive back home was delightfully uneventful.

Looking back on that adventure I am amazed at how calmly we handled challenge after challenge, never giving up our goal. We never argued. We just assumed that we would come up with a way over, under or through any obstacle that we encountered. Perhaps Jack would tell a different tale. We were close friends for several years after this. We attended each other's weddings. Then we drifted apart and have not been in touch for many years.

Sometimes I try to recapture that feeling I had the morning I got the flu, sitting there in the shelter with the snow falling. Somehow through the pain and the fog of fever I reached a place of complete, blissful surrender. There was nothing more I could do but wait till Jack woke up. If felt that we would somehow work things out and I might as well enjoy watching the snow falling on this special place at this special time.

Big Decision

It was a rare treat. My wife, Marty, and I were out having dinner at a quiet country inn, our first time out since the birth of our son eight months before. He was with a sitter. But this was more than a quiet meal. We had a major decision to make.

We were living on farm north of Philadelphia, renting one half of an old farm house and looking for a place to buy in the area. Finding one we could afford was proving to be most difficult. Just recently we got an offer from Marty's parents. They still owned the little house along the Whitewater River where Marty was raised. For the past thirteen years they had been renting it out to a family. That family had just moved out. If we wanted to make the move to Indiana we could rent it with an option to buy, but we had to decide soon. They didn't want it to sit empty.

There are two versions of what happened that night. Years later, when asked about the move, I said that Marty apparently slipped something into my wine. Because the next thing I remembered was awaking in the trunk of her car, bond and gagged, in some foreign land. Marty disputes this version, much like my mother did when Dad said that she threatened to jump off a bridge unless he married her.

The other version is that we decided, if either one of us found a job out there, we would make the move, and the other would stay home and take care of the kid. I let Marty go first. She was gone for a few days. When she returned she said she was offered a job. This was shocking news. She went out for an interview and I thought that, even if it went well, they would have to check references and she would probably need to return for a second interview. In the meantime, I would have to opportunity to set up some leads and go out to see what I could fine.

Now that option had suddenly been taken off the table, and I would become a stay at home dad, an occupation unheard of back in 1979. This was all happening much too fast.

Westward Ho!

I pulled the moving truck over to the side of the road when I saw Marty pull her car over just ahead of me. It was hot and it had already been a long day with very little progress. Our plan to drive all the way to our new home in Indiana in one day was already looking dubious.

The day before, with the help of friends, we packed all our earthly belongings into the big rental truck. This included a refrigerator and piano. It was a tight fit. Early this morning we took off. I was driving the truck following Marty in her little yellow Toyota

Rabbit. It was densely packed with house plants. Son, Brendan, now nine-months old, was in a car seat in the rear.

We got on the road and soon we got confused. I was supposed to be following Marty but somehow got ahead of her. I think she stopped for gas but I didn't see her do that and she didn't see me pass her. Since cell phones had yet to be invented, we had no way to communicate. When she got to the entrance to the PA Turnpike, she pulled over before getting on, waiting for me to catch up and wondering why I was taking so long.

She waited so long that she attracted the attention of the toll booth staff. A woman from the booth walked over to her and ask what was up. She told her that she was waiting for me, describing the truck. The woman said that truck when through the toll gate some time ago. Meanwhile, I was wondering why I lost sight of her and could not catch up. I pulled over at the first rest stop hoping to find her there. Seeing no sign of her, I was just about to get back on the pike when she pulled into the rest stop.

I followed her very closely after that. Now here we were, stopped again. I turned off the truck, got out and walked up to her car. She was in tears. She said that Brendan had been screaming and crying the entire trip, and now there was a funny noise coming from under the car. I looked under the vehicle and saw a pipe from the muffler dragging on the ground. So here we were, with our child and all our earthy belongings, stranded on the side of the road, wondering how things could get much worse. We soon found out.

I looked around and saw that we were right at the exit for Breezewood, Pa. A sign facing the turnpike invited us to "Breeze into Breezewood, the motel capital of the world." That seemed like a good idea, and I could think of no other option. It was a very hot day and neither vehicle had air conditioning. We would spend the night in an air-conditioned motel room. I would go looking for a garage to get the car fixed, and our son would be happily free from the confines of his car seat.

I walked back to the truck, climbed in and turned the key. The truck would not start. It sounded like it wanted to, but it just would not start. I walked back to the car and told Marty. We came up with a plan "B." I would drive with her to the toll booth. Hopefully they would have a phone I could use to call the truck rental company. She would go on to the nearest motel. We could see it from where we stood. I would walk back to the truck and wait for road service.

That plan worked. In about half an hour a service truck pulled up. The mechanic climbed into the truck and it started right up. He told me, as if I should have known, that the model truck I had would often not start back up once it heated up. All I had to do was wait for it to cool down.

I met up with Marty at the motel. Now I had to find a local mechanic to work on the car. I found one nearby. It was a father and son operation and they were getting ready to close up shop for the day. They were not very friendly, but they agreed to look at it. I expected the worse. My fate was in their hands and they would probably charge me a bunch of money and may have to get parts, which would delay our trip for a day or more.

They put it up on the lift, wired up the pipe, charged me a few bucks and told me it should last till I got to Indiana. Wow, what a relief. We had a relaxing night's sleep and pushed off in the morning. It was a long journey, but we made it without further incident.

While stranded there on the side of the road with my wife, child and all our earthy possessions, I thought about the pioneer families of long ago, making a similar journey west in search of a new home and opportunity. Perhaps when their horses overheated they just had to wait for them to cool down before starting again on their journey, just like my truck. While their goal was the same as ours, we certainly had advantages they would have appreciated, including an air-conditioned room in the motel capital of the world.

Transition

So here I was, spending weekdays at our new home with our nine-month old son, far away from the rest of my family and all my friends. It was not easy. My father-in law did his best to introduce me to the community. Jim was a country attorney with his own firm, established by his father before him. He was well known, well connected and well liked.

He would drive me all around the county, stopping often and without warning to tell me long stories about the particular spot where we were. Mostly, it seemed to me, these stops were in the middle of nowhere, along some narrow county road, surrounded by corn and soybeans. He might say that this was where Omer Prickle use to have several head of beef cows and a big red barn that burned down in 1961. Or was it 1962? No, it had to be 1961 because 1962 was the years Omer's son had his tractor accident and that definitely happened after the fire. I so wanted to make mental notes, thinking that all this may be important to my acceptance, but I struggled to stay awake.

He would take me to annual dinners of organizations such as the Kiwanis and the Chamber of Commerce, introducing me to farmers, business men, politicians and county officials. Inevitably, they would ask me what I did for a living. I tried to explain, but the conversation would always come to an abrupt end. They just didn't know how to respond. If I happened to run into one of them in town sometime later, they would ask me if I found a job yet. No, I wasn't even looking. I was raising a kid. It was no use explaining. They may have been more accepting if I told them that I was just waiting for the Rapture to come and take me to Heaven. My occupation was just so far beyond their level of understanding, and mine too, at times.

Then one evening I was talking to my father-in-law on the phone. He said that he heard that I had gotten a haircut that day. I was stunned. Do these people have nothing else to talk about? Back in Philly, as long as my parents did not get a call from the cops or the hospital, I could do just about anything I wanted with my time. Now, it seemed, I had no place to hide.

Brendan was a delightful child, for the first ten minutes of the day. For the rest of the day he was rambunctious and demanding, testing my endurance, a typical experience typically experienced by mothers. I found myself gravitating to any activity that would reestablish my masculinity. I learned to use a chain saw and sought any available opportunity to cut, chop and stack wood for our fireplace and wood burning furnace.

I yearned for any bit of adult conversation I could get, tuning into NPR whenever I could. Then one day it happened. I discovered the Phil Donahue Show on TV. If I turned the rabbit ears on top of our set just right I could see and hear an adult conversation about contemporary topics every weekday. Sometimes I could actually get Brendan down for a nap while the show was on. Then one day Phil had a show about an extraordinary new phenomenon in our culture. It seemed that some men were actually making the decision to stay home and raise their kids, giving up their traditional role as breadwinner. He had some of them on the show. He actually called them househusbands.

Judging from the reaction of his almost exclusively female audience, this was so strange that he could have been talking about men who had given birth to children or been abducted by aliens. But it gave me hope. Now I knew I was not alone. There were others out there somewhere that were like me. I now had a label, and I was a pioneer, forging a way that few men had gone before.

What in the heck is a Hoosier?

Nobody knows for sure how the label got associated with residents of Indiana, but there are many theories.

Some say there was once a Frenchman named Hoosier, a fur trader and lumberman, who hired many of the local men, and they became known as Hoosier's men. Another story is that, when someone came upon a cabin out here on the frontier, they would knock on the door and the occupant would say "Who's there?" in such a way that it sounded like "Hoosier."

But the one I like best, and so want to be true, has to do with a barroom brawl. Many years ago, before being tamed by the Lutherans, Baptist, Pentecostals and Catholics, this was a wild and unruly area. The struggle to survive resulted in much pent-up tension. Fortunately, for men, there was therapy available at the local tavern, aided by the copious consumption of moonshine.

During one such therapy session, some men got into a disagreement, which ended with one man cutting off the ear of another. The proprietor, seeing this as a learning opportunity, took the ear, put it in a jar with some alcohol he happened to have, and placed it on display on the back bar. Men would come in, look at it and ask "Who's ear?"

Sometimes I try to think of what it would have been like for me to have been in that bar on that night and have someone ask me what I did for a living. It could have been my ear there behind the bar.

On a more practical level, one definition of a Hoosier is a Kentuckian whose car broke down on the way to Detroit. This refers back to when the car industry in Detroit was booming and many folks migrated there from the south. The strange dialect spoken by the locals certainly supports this definition. The words "pin" and "pen" for instance, get the same pronunciation. You don't wash something, you whoosh it. You don't push something poosh it. The locals seem to jump on the first syllable of some works, misplacing the accent at the front. It isn't inSURance, it's INsurance. It's not umBRELla, it's UMbrella. A guitar is a GEtar. All this strange pronunciation was disconcerting at first, but I quickly got used to it. I just wish I could convince them that the proper (i.e.: Philadelphia) pronunciation of "water" is "wouder."

If you plan to go somewhere you will get there "Lord willing and the creek don't rise." When someone has unexpected success it just proves that "even a blind hog sometimes finds an acorn"

On my first trip to the local grocery for a few items, I encountered a problem at the check-out counter. I could not understand most of what the cashier was saying, but I was able to fake it, nodding and chuckling when she appeared to say something funny. But then she looked directly at me and asked "Deyawanasick?" My jaw dropped and I said "What?"

She asked me again, seeming slightly annoyed. I saw she was reaching for a bag and figured out that she was asking me if I wanted a sack. I resisted the urge to tell her that, where I come from, they are bags, and what she was drinking was not pop but soda.

When my father-in law took me to one of the annual dinners (Chamber of Commerce, I think) I was sitting across from a state representative. We struck up a conversation. The room was noisy and it was hard for us to hear each other. At one point he looked at me and said "Please?"

I waited for him to complete the sentence: please pass the salt, please pass the biscuits, or some such request. But that was it. Just "Please" hanging out there in the air and waiting for a response. He did this a few more times and I was convinced he had some sort of disability, some cognitive processing problem perhaps. Later I learned that this was a common response from Cincinnatians when they did not hear what you said. He was asking me to please repeat myself.

I learned that he was originally from Ohio, which is very close to my new home town. His family was part of a second wave of migration, more recent that Kentucky migration. In contrast to the Kentuckians, the Buckeyes seem to be wealthier, seeking cheap land to build fancy homes. Both migrations continue to this day, though the Kentuckian has slowed to a trickle. And there is a bit of a reverse migration, a return to the hills and hollers of the Bluegrass State.

Many of locals with Kentucky roots I have met are proud of their roots and feel right at home in the hills and hollers of Southeast Indiana, which is not at all like the flatlands a bit to the north. They feel they have moved up in the world. From hillbilly to cliffwilliam.

In the fall, a woman from Kentucky told me about a whore house that was in town. She went on and on about it. I was appalled. Then she said it was sponsored by the Kiwanis (or Lions, or some such civic group). I was astounded. I knew this could not be correct. I questioned her more carefully and found out she was talking about a "horror" house that was set up for Halloween. I'm relieved to know she was not talking about a whore house. That sure would give a different twist to trick-or-treat.

I used to think that one sign of a civilized community was the existence of a subway train system, but I have given up that notion. Now I think that a truly functioning community needs to have an equal number of bars and churches, a healthy balance of sin and redemption. I look around my new community and think we are doing rather well in this respect.

The Cow in the Middle of the Road

The little house we moved into in Indiana was known to the locals as Mullin's Camp. It was built as a recreational spot along the Whitewater River many years ago by my wife's grandfather. Her parents put on a small addition to accommodate their addition of four daughters and named it Riverwood. The Whitewater River is the fastest flowing river in Indiana. After the devastating flood of 1959, the family moved to higher ground, building a home on top of the wooded hill directly across the road from Riverwood.

One warm spring day I was getting ready to paint the side of the house facing the road. Marty was inside with our toddler son and infant daughter. I looked up and saw a big, brown cow standing in the middle of the narrow two-lane county road right next to the house. The house sits below the road, so the roof of the house is about level with the road, about twenty feet away. The house is halfway through a horseshoe bend in the road, so a car coming from either direction would not see the beast until it was too late. The hill across the road was a steep climb. The ramifications were too much for me to ignore. I would either witness a car-cow collision or have a vehicle leave the road to avoid the cow and end up on my house.

With encouragement from Marty, I climbed up to the road and cautiously approached the animal. It did not move. I shouted and waved. It did not move. I jumped up and down and made horrible faces and threatening gestures. It did not move. It just stood there, perfectly still. It was facing the house so that it would be hit broadside by a car coming from either direction. I tried reasoning with it. It did not move.

Having been born and raised a city boy, I never before faced such a situation. In fact, I had never had occasion to get so close to a cow, nor had any desire to do so. But fortunately, I was also raised on a steady diet of cowboy shows on television and at the neighborhood movie theater. I particularly liked Roy Rogers and my siblings will tell you that my identification with good ole Roy bordered on the pathological. Somehow, I knew all those years of watching Roy battle the bad guys and fight for justice was not a waste of time. It was all preparing me for this very moment. I was meant to be a hero like Roy, pulling out a victory for justice from the very jaws of disaster at the very last moment. I learned all about cows from the silver screen. I could do this. I could save this cow.

I sprang into action immediately. In the basement, I found a sizable length of thick rope that I fashioned into a lasso. I went back up to the road and lassoed the beast on my very first attempt. Then I tugged and tugged and tugged. It did not move. Just as I was wrapping the rope around my hand to get a better grip, I heard a vehicle coming. It sounded like it was moving fast. Suddenly the cow turned and started running up the hill through the woods. The rope instantly tightened around my hand so I could not let go.

I was pulled up and through the woods as an old pickup truck went roaring by just behind me. I ran hard so I would not fall down and be dragged along. After several terrifying moments, I saw the beast up ahead of me get tangled around a tree and fall. I was able to release the rope from my hand. I rubbed my purple fingers trying to get some circulation back in my hand. Then I heard the sound. I had never heard anything like it. I looked up and saw that the cow was struggling for breath and bellowing deep, mournful howls through its constricted throat. It was plaintive and eerie, and chilled me to the bone. The noose was tight on its neck. The rope was wrapped around a tree just high enough to begin strangling the cow when it fell.

I wondered what the penalty was for lynching a cow. Had this ever been done before? How much was the creature worth? Would I have to pay for pain and suffering? Would I be labeled for life as the man who lynched the cow and be ostracized by my new community? Then I realized that I had my trusty old jack knife in my pocket. I knew what I must do. I took the knife from my pocket and cautiously approached the beast. Its eyes were bulging. It was foaming at the mouth. Its tongue was hanging out and to the side of its huge, gaping, ugly mouth. The tongue seemed to be about two feet long. The howls had stopped and it was now making horrible guttural sounds. I had to get right up to the head of the disgusting creature and cut away at the rope at its neck. It seemed to take forever, but finally I cut through. The beast collapsed and began to catch its breath.

I returned to the house and told Marty what had happened. She thought we should call around to neighbors to see if we could find out who owned the cow. I wanted no part of that. I was through with the cow. I just wanted to get the incident behind me. I certainly didn't want to explain to anyone what had happened. After a while, I went out across the road and up the hill a bit. I could see that it was gone. Perhaps it had learned a lesson. Don't ever take a walk down near the house where the mad urban cowboy lives.

This all happened many years ago, but I still think about that cow from time to time. I can't understand how it just appeared on the road so suddenly and how it disappeared so mysteriously. For some time after the incident I carefully checked the local paper, which was prone to report such things as attempted cow lynching for lack of more important news in our sleepy little town. I kept my ears open when talking to folks in town or at county functions. I waited for the phone call asking me if I knew anything about an incident of bovine abuse occurring near my house. I feared I had left finger prints on the cow.

I never heard a single word about it. One theory I have is that the cow was from another county or state and was zapped up into an alien spaceship for examination and then carelessly returned to the wrong place. When the aliens saw what a tragedy the cow faced at the hands of the demented earthling they realized their mistake and rescued it after I left it. Perhaps there is a simpler explanation. I'm just grateful we both survived the encounter. Perhaps the cow would have gotten out of the way of the speeding truck without my intervention, but then again maybe I did get it to move. We certainly did avoid a disastrous collision at the last possible moment, and I did save its life by cutting the rope. I think Roy would have been proud of me.

Near Miss

I still shutter whenever I think about it. I was busy splitting firewood outside our little house on the river when my wife called from the kitchen window, "Get Meghan!"

I had been watching our toddler daughter and her brother carefully, or so I thought, being sure they kept a safe distance from my work. I looked around and saw her way up the lane, almost to the road. I was amazed that such a little child, still on wobbly legs, could move so quickly. Then I heard the sound of a car racing toward the blind curve. Surely the driver would be unable to stop in time.

There are moments in every life when things can go tragically wrong, and sometimes they do. Deep guilt and regret often follow sorrow, adding to the pain of loss. Fortunately, we dodged the bullet this time. I raced up the lane as I shouted out to her. I picked her up and carried her back to the house as the car hurried by. The driver was oblivious to what may have happened.

When I see her now, all grown up and off on her own, I often think of that day. How could I have been so careless? What would our lives have been like without her? How could we have possibly recovered?

All those precious moments we had together as she grew up would never have happened. It is strange that I can feel so guilty about something that did not happen, yet I do. There are probably things I should feel guilty about that I am totally unaware of, or simply don't see as my fault. Guilt can be such a powerful motivator, yet those who should not feel it often do, and those who should feel it often don't.

Every time I recall this incident Meghan gets closer to the road. The car gets closer to her and travels at a faster speed. They get so close to each other that I feel the breeze of the car as I snatch her up just as the car goes whizzing by.

Mini Basketball

One day my son came home from first grade with a parent permission slip for mini basketball. He wanted to play, and the slip included a box to check for a parent who would be willing to help coach. I checked the box and wrote "Only if you can't find anyone else." I was called the next day, and the following weekend I found myself in the local school gymnasium.

I was a recent transplant to the Hoosier state. Born and raised in the metropolis of Philadelphia,

Pennsylvania, I was still adjusting to the strange ways of our newly adopted small rural town, and still trying to shake off my east coast snobbery. Back then I still told friends that, when I moved from Pennsylvania to Indiana, I raised the average IQ of both states considerably. I don't say that anymore.

I looked around the gym, buzzing with activity, full of rambunctious little boys and their watchful fathers. In the middle of it all was the high school coach, Gary. He was an enthusiastic guy with a positive and friendly attitude. All the men seemed to know one another and know all the boys, their families and grandparents. I knew no one.

These were the days when basketball was still king in the state and Hoosier hysteria was a force to be reckoned with, where every town and hamlet rallied around the high school team. When the crops were put away, and the air turned cold, and the brutal winter winds swept across the plains, there was little left to do but struggle to stay warm and root the local boys on to victory through the sectionals and the regionals, and perhaps, just maybe, the semi-state and finals, a single-class system filled with David and Goliath struggles. Rarely did the little guy win, but when he did it was accompanied by an outpouring of human emotion equal to any sports upset in the world. It was enough to give any small-town hope that it too, with firm dedication and determination, could defeat the big teams from the big cities. Coach Gary saw mini basketball as the early development of the raw material that would get Brookville to the state championship someday.

When Gary phoned me about coaching I said that I did not want to coach my own son. I wanted Brendan to have a coach that wasn't his dad, to experience the guidance of a different adult male. To my surprise, Gary liked the idea and made it a rule that no father would have his own son on his team. The other dad coaches seemed to like or at least accept the idea. We ran the kids through drills, watched them, and took turns picking kids for our teams. The baskets were lowered and rules modified. We had a week or two for practice before the season begun.

It was clear to me from day one that the other coaches knew a lot more about coaching the game than I did, and they took it all quite seriously. They were good at correcting kids and getting them to learn. When my kids goofed up I was too easy on them. I just told them it was ok, just try again. I was more of a cheer leader than a coach. During one time-out, I knelt on one knee to talk with my boys. They gathered around me and Michael, one of the smaller boys, came up and sat on my knee. He grew up and became an attorney.

Then the season began and we started winning, and winning, and winning. I am as convinced today as much as I was then that I had little to do with this. I got the feeling the other coaches agreed, but they just could not figure it out. We got into the playoffs and then to the championship game, against my son's team. It was a tie game at halftime and I gave a dramatic and stirring inspirational speech to my boys. Then I asked if they had any questions. Bobby raised his hand and asked, "Can we go home now?" We won by one point.

I coached mini basketball three more years – second, third and fourth grades. We won the championship one of those years and lost in close championship finals the other two. After the first grade, we allowed fathers to have their own sons on their team and I did get to coach Brendan. The fourth year started off with a major scandal. Coach Gary was caught having an affair with another school employee. Both were married. Gary had two sons. The younger one was a mini basketball super star in my son's class. When confronted, Gary resigned. He and his family quickly left the community. This all happened very suddenly. I got the news about this one day while Brendan was still in school. I struggled with how to explain to him when he got home. I was both relieved and surprised when Brendan told me he knew all about it. Apparently, the community grapevine had tentacles all the way down to the fourth grade. He seemed unfazed by the news. I realized then that the life of a fourth grader was filled with far more urgent and immediate concerns than the dalliances of adults.

Some years later, Indiana adopted a highly contentious class system, improving the odds of a small-town team ending the season at the top of their division, while eliminating the possibility of a little school from a little town bumping off a big city powerhouse for the state title. Something is lost and something is gained. In 1954 the Milan Indians, with a school enrollment of 161 students beat the mighty and highly favored Muncie Central Bearcats to claim the Indiana State High School Basketball Title. The little town of Milan erupted in ecstasy. Their boys had reached the pinnacle of success, bringing an outpouring of pride and euphoria to the community. Such an accomplishment will never happen again in Indiana. But life goes on. Men still gather with their little sons on frosty Saturday mornings in the local gym for mini basketball. Women and girls gather to pursue their dreams of glory as well.

Perhaps my son learned something from the mini basketball experience. I still ponder what, if anything, I did. He never became a basketball star. I never became a famous coach. We got through it together. We still remain friends. Much is made of the importance of sports in building character. The older I get the more I prefer cooperation to competition. I do not know whatever happen to Gary and his family. Perhaps they found a way to work through his transgression of the marital vow and they are now living happily ever after. I hope so. I do know that life sometimes takes unexpected turns. Sometimes it is best to respond with a full court press. Sometimes you just need to call a time out. Knowing what to do when the time comes is the art of living.

The Plunge

Once again, I was outside splitting firewood when this happened. It was morning on a New Year's Day. Our house guests, good friends June and Walt, were inside with their two boys, Marty and our kids. We had all spent New Year's Eve together as we typically did. Our guests spent the night and were getting ready to head home.

Meghan, the youngest of the kids, was nine years old at the time. She came running out of the house to tell me she was going to participate in the Polar Bear Plunge.

The Plunge is an annual event that defies reason. Participants jump into frigid water in the winter. It is a tradition in many places in the world. The local event was held up at the lake at the spillway, where the lake water flows from the dam. It was a popular event for many years, drawing folks from near and far.

Why do they do this? The desire to do something completely irrational, seeking a thrill, seems to be deeply imbedded in the human psyche. I understand this. Exposing your body to extreme situations can be exhilarating. Meeting the challenge and overcoming the danger can be thrilling and rewarding. It can also be tragic.

I told her it was much too cold for this and she should go talk to her mother. She told me she already had done that and ran back into the house. I was baffled by this. It could not be. Marty is always more logical and practical than I am. She would not approve of our daughter being involved. I was still trying to make sense of this when everyone poured out of the house and quickly loaded into two cars. They were in a hurry, they explained, to get to the lake in time. Our guests would stop and watch the plunge on their way back home.

I quickly realized that none of the others were going to participate in the plunge. When Meghan hit the water, she might panic. Someone needed to be there with her, and that someone had to be me. I rushed into the house, stripped down, put on a bathing suit I somehow managed to find in the back of my closet, put my coveralls back on, hopped into my truck and raced to the starting point.

I got there just in the nick of time. Fortunately, I had no time to fret over what I was about to do. I just had to react and I did. Meghan and I waded into the water together. Somehow, we made it across the spillway and got back again, fulfilling the requirement to be officially proclaimed a Polar Bear. The first thing I noticed when I got out of the water was the unusual condition of my skin. Every pore was filled with frozen water. When I touched my arm, it was crunchy. Everywhere I touched was crunchy. I stood there for a moment in amazement, then it hit me. I was really cold! I accepted the towels offered to me, dried off the best I could and climbed back into my coveralls.

A few years later Meghan wanted to do it again. That time she was on her own.

The Cat and the Gig

When son Brendan came home from Oberlin College for Christmas 2000 he brought a friend; a stray cat he and his housemate adopted. They had given this female feline the comfort of their house and a name, Bill Evans. Now Bill became quite happy with central heating and much preferred the indoors to the outside in this very cold winter in the very cold northern college town. But at our family home we do not allow animals inside due to allergies and the general mess they create. We have had many animals that do quite well outside, living in our detached garage complete with pet door, or in a doghouse. We have found that once a cat or dog is introduced to the inside of a house it is very difficult for the animal to readjust to living outside. This was the problem Bill faced. Unbeknownst to her, she would be living in the cold garage for a week, in this very cold winter.

The first morning after the first night of this experience I was the first up to go off to work. It was still dark. I called to the cat in the garage and got a response, a plaintive meow. I tried to locate her but could not. First the sound was right in front of me, and then it came from another area of the three-car garage. I went here and there wading through tools and mowers and around vehicles. I could not find the beast. It was like the Cheshire cat in <u>Alice Through the Looking Glass</u>, only without the smile. I was afraid to start my truck, thinking that it may have found its way under the hood. Once upon a time I gave a kitten a fateful ride on my fan belt when it crawled up under my hood for the warmth of the engine. I didn't want to puree Bill, but I had to get to work. I started up the truck, backed it out, and walked back to the garage to again try to find Bill. I called and called but got no answer, not a sound. I checked for a trail of blood from the garage to the hood of my truck. I was relieved to find none.

There was no sign of the cat that day or that night. The next day we were all off for the holidays. Brendan was playing the piano downstairs when the cat appeared behind him, just outside the balcony door. As we got Bill settled and fed, Brendan told us that the cat often came to the door when he played piano back at college. Brendan had a baby grand piano and an outside door in his bedroom at school (no room for a bed, he slept under the piano). Over the next few days we learned that Bill spent most of her time in the rafters of the garage, while mice played below. She gradually adapted, while the temperature remained well below freezing.

Brendan had a gig for New Year's Eve. He was to play keyboard in a big band in the main ballroom of the Hilton Hotel in downtown Akron, Ohio. So, midday on December 31st he packed up to go. He planned to drive the five-hour trip back to his college house. There he would change into his tux and head to the gig. He managed to get Bill out of the rafters, and headed off. Later that afternoon we got a call from him saying that he made it, but had a problem. When he pulled up to his house the cat was so excited to be back that she was out the door of the car before Brendan even had it open all the way. When they entered the house, they found that the furnace was off and the house was freezing. No one had been there for about a week, so there was no telling how long the furnace had been down. Fortunately, the pipes were not frozen. He called the landlady, who called a repairman who promised to be there at 6 pm. Brendan had a long trip to Akron, so he needed to leave soon after the repairman arrived.

We were sitting at breakfast New Year's Day when he called us with the rest of the story. The repairman came and quickly got the furnace fixed.

Brendan set the thermostat and left for the gig. He got to Akron but had a problem finding the hotel. He ended up going the wrong way on a one-way street and was stopped by two young cops. They had a friendly exchange and the cops admitted that the street signs were confusing. They then asked if they could search his car. Having nothing to hide, he said yes. He was concerned that this delay would make him late for the gig, but it took just six minutes for them to complete the task. They gave him directions to the hotel and he was again on his way.

He had traveled but a few blocks when he realized that the cops never gave him his driver's license back. He found a gas station with a pay phone, but had no coins in his tux pockets. The mechanic let him use the garage phone and he called the police station. They drove to the gas station and returned his license. He got to the gig with little time to spare.

He said that the band was fine and well-liked by the party of "yuppies who didn't know how to dance." He got back to his house at about 4am and opened the door to a blast of very hot air. The thermostat was stuck and the furnace ran the whole time he was gone. The temperature was over 90 degrees. He fiddled with it and got it to turn off. He stripped off all his clothes and got to sleep.

Being a parent means opening your life to the endless adventures of your children. You cry, you laugh and sometimes you just have to shake your head in disbelief. Occasionally a true gem of a story comes along, one you can actually tell others without sounding prideful or without embarrassment. This story seems to fit this category, and is a good one to start the new millennium. It has a happy ending and no one was hurt, but I somehow can't help but wondering what Bill Evans thought about all of this.

Thanksgiving Flatulence

It was a year before the turn of the last century that this curious event took place. When Marty's parents moved to a retirement community, we bought the big house they lived in on top of the hill. With the purchase came the responsibility and honor of hosting the annual Thanksgiving gathering of the Mullin clan, wife Marty's people. They come from far and wide, from states north and south and east and west. Some arrive early in the week and some stay through the weekend. We have a home full of guests morning, noon and night.

Weather permitting, we spend a lot of time outside, hiking the hills and creek beds in search of fossils. We toss Frisbees and footballs and play a variety of games. There are warm fires, good conversations and of course lots of good food and drink. After Thanksgiving dinner, we gather around the piano for an evening of music and song, accompanied by an assortment of instruments. We usually have about twenty-five guests: Marty's sisters, their spouses, their kids, our kids, a cousin or two and significant others. Marty's mother, Mary, the matriarch, was about eighty-five at this time.

We also get visitors from foreign lands who have some association with a family member. This year we had a visiting scientist from Pakistan who was observing Ramadan. Since she fasted till sundown we had our Thanksgiving meal a bit later than usual. As the meal ended I was feeling a wee bit tired. The hubbub of transitional activities, from meal to music, was underway. Our two-butt kitchen was full of folks eager to help with the clean-up. I was clearly not needed and unnoticed so I took the opportunity to take a little respite. This transition from clean-up to music enjoyment would take a while, and I just wanted to stretch out on my bed alone for a few minutes.

The dark bedroom was inviting and it appeared my wife's side of the bed was heaped up with blankets and spreads. I slipped in on my side, took a deep breath and enjoyed a moment of peace and emotional distance from the festivities. I stretched out, took a deep breath and felt a familiar sensation, deep in my bowels. From the moment it started I knew this was going to be something special, a fitting tribute to the fine meal and all the hands that put it on the table. Anxious with anticipation I focused on relaxing and letting it flow.

It started with a musical note somewhere just south of middle C, accompanied by a rising rush of aromas, slightly pungent yet intriguing, the sweet soprano of cranberry and the savory bass notes of turkey and gravy. I detected a hint of chardonnay and pumpkin pie filling out the spaces of a musical and aromatic symphony, rising, ever rising, reaching and releasing, I let it all go, appreciating every subtle movement. It seemed to go on forever and I did not want it to stop. I was overwhelmed by a feeling of contentment as the experience ended and the complex vapors filled the room. I inhaled deeply to recapture the experience. All was right. All was good.

Then it happened. The pile of blankets next to me started to move. Then the face of my mother-in-law appeared close to my own. "Aren't you cold?" she asked.

There are moments in life when worlds collide with such suddenness that it is difficult to adjust. This should not, could not be happening. But alas it was. I sprung from the bed and hurled myself from the room, muttering vague and disjointed apologies.

Some embarrassing moments are just too embarrassing to talk about. Others are too good not to tell. We all make mistakes. We try to forget and move on, but sometimes the aromas linger. I could spend a lot of time thinking about how stupid it was of me not to have noticed her under the pile of blankets. But she was a frail little woman. She lived on for many more years, blessed with a keen and inquisitive mind. We never spoke about this event, but often when I visited with her I could not help wondering if she remembered that night as vividly as I do.

Ski Notes

I awoke to new snow on top of old. I slipped into my second winter skin (coveralls) and cross-country ski boots and headed out to the pond. High Acres, the name of the field south of the house, was a pristine, glistening canvas. The trails I made yesterday were covered in the night, so I was starting over. Where should I begin? I pushed off across the field, around the golden raintree and straight across to the conifers, roughly parallel to the lane. The snow was crunchy on top and slick underneath. A core sample would reveal each of the past several days in clear layers, a stratified record of the ice, wind and snow.

The skis glided smoothly. The morning air was brisk. It was dead president's day, and my third straight day of cross-country skiing, warm fires, homemade soup and bread. I decided to remake the cardio-course first, straight across the field to the crab apple, and back along the majestic pines. After several times around, it was slick and fast, providing quite a workout.

I made tracks that crossed each other and some that intersected and ran together for a bit. It was great fun and got me thinking about other tracks, ones from my past. When I was a kid my dad would put up

173

train tracks every year on Christmas Eve, waiting until all seven of his kids were in bed. He'd set them up on a platform in the basement. The display had trestles, tunnels, and switch-tracks, along with houses, a post office, a church, and various other buildings; all lit up with Christmas lights strung under the platform and poking up through carefully cut holes. I recall great adventures with the little plastic people who often ended up on the tracks just as the engine came around the bend and picked up speed.

We had a little bottle with a dropper in the cap. A few drops in the smoke stack of the engine would produce gentle puffs of smoke good enough for a complete round trip. I don't think this fun ever lasted for more than a day or two each year. Inevitably someone would neglect to lower the throttle on the transformer as the train came down from the trestle and into the turn at maximum speed. It would fly off the track, off the platform and crash on the concrete floor. The train adventures would be over until the next year, a short-lived pleasure like the snows of February.

I got into a rhythm on my skis, picking up steam and the years peeled away. I felt myself holding fast to my father's hand as we looked down from a bridge to watch the circus train pull into the central Philadelphia station. This was a ritual Dad tried to bring back from his childhood with tales of wild animals riding by in cages. I hoped to see the long neck of a giraffe sticking out of a hole in the roof of the caboose. We saw nothing but a long train slowly snaking its way into the station.

My heart pumped hard. I slowed to rest. Then I decided to make more trails. I glided along the Quiet Walk, through a grove of huge pines that rise and come together like the walls and ceiling of a great cathedral, a place that seems holy and fitting for meditation. My mind went to timeless places and the snow was rich with metaphor. I pumped through life and time, each turn a calculated risk. It's good to keep aware of what is just ahead, what is far ahead, and what is under foot.

I exited the cathedral at the east side of the pond. Then went down the bank around the house, startling the birds at the feeders, out through the gate and down to Windy Knob. This was top speed. Remembering how to stop and judging when I had gone far enough was important. Too much too fast and I could go over the knob. The hillside trees would prevent me from ending up in the river, but not the emergency room. I manipulated the skis just right but I was going too fast. I planned to fall and did, safely.

Marty had a cold but felt well enough today to get out and ski. I saw her pass from atop the tractor as I plowed the lane. We had been ice-bound and snow-bound for over two days now. It was wonderful. Later we skied off together across the hilltop fields, accompanied by Samba, the neighbor's large white husky. We skied home, built a fire and heated some soup. The beans and turkey, homegrown tomatoes and spices had been getting to know each other for a few days. Beans were soaked overnight and cooked up much of yesterday. Then we got the phone call. Schools would be closed tomorrow. So would the federal government.

The earth still spins on its axis and soon enough we would be back into our normal life pace. Spring would come and there would be grass to cut and gardens to tend. This had been a magical time for us. Night fell and the wine was fine. Tomorrow would bring what it would bring.

Country lessons

Things I've learned about living in the country:

- Don't offer zucchinis to others in late-summer. They already have plenty. Zucchini season is the only time some people lock their doors.

- The difference between a Franklin County farmer and a crow is that a crow can leave a deposit on a John Deere.

- Don't think you're Roy Rogers and lasso the cow in the middle of the road, which gets frighten by a car and runs up the hill through the woods, which wouldn't be so bad except you have the rope wrapped around your hand and you get pulled up the hill by the cow.

- Try not to look too much like a city boy. Just because you live in the same place in the country for a quarter century doesn't mean you belong there. Lineage helps, and you better behave yourself. Homeland security here predates 9/11. People will know about what you do.

- Squirrels, raccoons and many other creatures are smarter than people. No human scale of intelligence can measure this.

- Coyotes make alluring communal howls in the night and have a vertical leap of about 14 inches that they can do on a trot while chasing your dogs. Deer and turkey families hold equal rights to the pond, but neither has rights to the garden.

- The language is not so hard to understand except in certain cases when they forget who you are and speak in dialect (Kentuckian), and make repeated references to people and events as though you should know.

Critters

I awoke at 5am and could smell skunk in the thick, cool air that seeped in through the window. I'm home alone. Marty is off for the long Memorial Day weekend, visiting family and attending a nephew's high school graduation. I wanted to go back to sleep, but I just had to check the have-a-heart trap I set last night to catch another one of the raccoons that have been terrorizing our flowerbeds and bird feeders.

I caught one on my first try a few nights ago. It was big and angry and tried to lunge at me through the cage. The bumpy ride in the back of the pickup truck took the wind out of him. My destination was a property we own several miles away. We call it Indian Creek. By the time we got there the coon was disoriented and docile, but able to take off like a bat out of hell when I opened the trap. Raccoons are easy, I thought. But what if I catch a skunk in the trap?

Sharing similar lifestyles and interest, skunks and raccoons enjoy similar nighttime pleasures, and are both likely to be attracted to my bait. If I get a skunk in the trap, I'm told that I need to quietly approach it holding an old blanket or burlap tarp in front of me, and slowly drape it over the trap. Skunks like to see the target before they spray, so they say. Then I need to slowly lift the cage, gently place it in the pickup, and navigate the hills and hollers of Franklin County without upsetting the critter.

When I get there, I need to gently move the cage to the ground and open the trap, a task that takes two hands and requires me to lean over the cage. I can't imagine how I could do all this without getting sprayed. Perhaps I should disguise myself as a mama skunk.

Our neighbor once caught one live and just shot it right through the cage. The dying critter sprayed. The trap was too close to his house and his windows were open. He doesn't like to talk about it much, but you can coax the story out of his young daughters, who tell it with eyes of mischief, giggling like cow birds.

The striped skunk's anal glands hold about a tablespoon of a fetid, oily, yellowish musk. Ironically this musk is used to make perfume for humans, valued for its clinging properties. Somehow, of course, they get the skunk stink out before putting another stink in.

With that one tablespoon of liquid the skunk can jet spray five or six times, each time for ten to fifteen feet. The mist may reach three times as far, and the smell can carry a mile. The smell seems to linger forever.

I got out of bed and made my way through the dark house to the door, where I could peek out at the trap. It was out on the patio, about four feet away. Yes, it was sprung and there was a critter inside, but it was too dark for me to see what it was.

Some agrarian naturalists might view our relationship with nature as a constant war against everything that is out there to get us or is in the way of our comfort and progress. Natural stuff is the enemy which must be dominated and exploited to satisfy our appetites. Others believe we should live in harmony with nature, accepting our place in the natural world and seeking to understand and accommodate.

I got out the flashlight and, through the dark and milky morning, could just barely make out the mask of a raccoon. I went back through the dark house and flopped on the bed, on my back, limbs spread, relieved but unable to sleep, waiting for the light of dawn.

In an attempt to define a just war, the US Catholic Conference in 1993 said "Force may be used only to correct a grave evil, i.e., aggression or massive violation of basic human rights of whole populations." But what of war on non-humans? Does anything go? It seems we have been fighting a war on other life forms since before our emergence from the primordial sea, with little concern for any rules. Yet pesky nature keeps coming back to bite us.

On my way to Indian Creek, just before the turn for the creek bed, I came across a huge dead raccoon in the middle of the road. Such road kill is a common site. Was this the one I had dropped of the day before? Was the one I had now, smaller and more docile, its mate? I pictured helpless babies left alone it the woods. Perhaps coyotes would get them to feed their young. Soon the avian highway crew, consisting mainly of crows and vultures, would be out to clean the carcass from the road. They will work efficiently and effectively and will be followed by insects so nothing will go to waste. They work for food and require no pension or health care benefits. The release of the raccoon went smoothly and I returned home to find a pair of Canada geese, with three young chicks, taking up residence by our pond, a clear violation of the goose treaty of 2004, which is purely a figment of my imagination.

Canada geese are elegant looking creatures and the yellow chicks are so cute. I try not to do cute. It usually gets me in trouble. I tolerated a goose family a few years ago and soon found that even a small family can produce large quantities of poop. Their digestive systems work rapidly, so the bird can be light enough for flight. I once saw a flock of them walking across a field eating and pooping at an equally rapid pace. They seem to poop everywhere. Getting them off the pond is difficult and usually requires two people, one for each side of the pond, walking along, hooting, yelling and waving threateningly until they fly off. With just one person, they just swim to the other side.

I managed to get between them and the pond while they were resting on the grass in the shade. I waved a broom, attempting to herd them away from the property. Since the chicks were too young to fly, mom became protective and dad defensive. Mom led the way, followed by the chicks, rushing and stumbling, trying to keep up. Dad brought up the rear, squawking and becoming more threatening by the minute.

Mom made a turn at the drive and headed right to our house. She tried to go around the house, but had to get over the railroad ties that line the parking area. She was able to do this but the chicks were not. They tried to jump, but ended up in a pile. At this point dad had enough. Broom or no broom, this mad human had to go. He stalked toward me with remarkable fierceness and determination.

The moment of truth had come. I knew that, if I backed down even the slightest it would be all over. I'd end up fleeing down over the hill and seeking refuge in town. Marty would come home to find geese feasting in our pantry and sleeping in our bed. We looked each other in the eye. Just then I heard the now familiar squawk of momma goose. Both daddy goose and I turned at the same time to see that she had somehow gotten the chicks over the ties. Dad turned to go after them and the moment of confrontation was over.

We continued on around the house and I got them across the field and over the hill into the woods.

I returned to the house to cool off. That night in bed, as I was trying to get to sleep, I kept thinking about raccoons, skunks, geese and other critters. How do we peacefully coexist with the deer that ravish our gardens and the squirrels that feast at our bird feeders? What if I do find a skunk in the trap in the morning? I thought for certain I would wake to see the geese floating happily again on the pond.

Before dawn I rose and shined a light on the trap. Two sets of eyes stared back at me. Remarkably, two juvenile raccoons got caught together. The opening to the trap is narrow. The first one in should have sprung the trap, leaving the second outside. Even though they were small, I could not see how they could have passed through the opening shoulder to shoulder.

I put the trap in the truck and headed out the drive. There were no geese on the pond and I had no skunk to deal with. The day was starting out fine.

The Visitor

He showed up on the morning of my sixtieth birthday and just sat there at the edge of the yard, looking up at the house. He seemed to be looking right at me. I've seen coyotes before, but not one behaving

184

like this one. Usually I see them prancing across the meadow, headed somewhere and anxious to get there. I hear them howling at night and once saw them chasing our dogs. This one just sat there in the open and stared up at me as though he had something to say or something to ask or something he wanted from me.

The neighbors have livestock and they don't much care for coyotes. They shoot them when they come near. I tell the neighbors to chase them my way. I have no livestock. For me the coyotes are the perfect substitute for pets. They chase the deer and the rabbits and other varmints away from our vegetable gardens and I don't have to feed them or take them to the vet. But this one, in a manner of speaking, was an odd duck. And maybe it had been a duck at one time.

In American Indian lore the coyote is often portrayed as a shape-shifter, capable of taking on the form of other creatures. Sometimes he is thought of as a trickster or a joker, but he is also revered as a messenger of personal transformation through self-reflection. A coyote sighting could be a sign to lighten up and not take life too seriously, and a reminder that whatever we do to others will come right back at us. A coyote sighting could be a warning to turn around and go in a different direction. Was this beast visiting on this particular day trying to deliver a birthday message, or was this just an odd occurrence with no message at all? It must be the latter I thought.

It often occurs to me as odd that we find special significates in birthdays that are multiples of five. Why do we take age sixty as more significant that age fifty-nine for instance? Are our brains hardwired to think in such a way? The only exceptions seem to be age sixteen and age twenty-one. Why is that? Who is to say at what age we are suddenly able to drive a motor vehicle, drink alcohol or vote? When does one officially get to be a geezer? It all seems so arbitrary. Birthdays measure the passage of time, but what is time? Einstein said that the dividing line between past, present and future is an illusion. So, reality is really timeless. I stared out at the coyote. He offered no opinion.

We were hosting several visitors from out of state this day. They were not coming for my birthday. It was just a coincidence, like the presence of the coyote I suppose. I had to attend to hosting duties. I broke eye contact with the creature, or spirit or whatever it was. Yes, I believe we had actually connected eye to eye. I blinked first. I checked back on him from time to time. He remained sitting in the same spot. I watched him preen himself meticulously, licking his paws and scrubbing his body, behind his ears and over his haunches.   Each time he seemed to sense me watching and would glare back. Our human guests took interest in our canine visitor as well, also finding it odd.

Mark Twain had a lesser opinion of the coyote than the American Indian did. He wrote that the coyote was "... a living, breathing allegory of Want. He is always hungry. He is always poor, out of luck and friendless."

But our visitor didn't look like that at all. He seemed at ease and confident, well-groomed and well fed. Perhaps he had just finished off a rabbit. The coyote Sam Clemens encountered in the desert on his journey west was most likely living under more trying circumstances. Our hills are alive with little critters that make fine meals.

Just before we sat down to our meal I looked out the window one more time. The coyote was gone. But a crow flew across the sky.

Hmmm!

Turkey fight

One fine day I looked out and saw two, big male turkeys fighting down at the edge of the yard. One had its head totally inside the mouth of the other, where it seemed to be stuck. They pushed each other back and forth. This went on for several minutes. I wondered how this was going to end.

We see these birds around the house often, but never before like this. It the spring the males display and strut about, reminding me of the mummers in the New Year's Day parade back in Philly. The hens mostly ignore them, preferring to peck around under the bird feeders. The gobblers fight over the females and for dominance of the flock. They are equipped for battle with strong wings, strong beaks and sharp spurs. Bedecked with wattles and snoods, they are a frightening site. They have a rigid pecking order, enforced by both Tom's and hens. Sex is not always consensual.

Like many birds, turkeys peck at their reflection in our windows. The competitor they see there is always an equal match. No matter how hard they try, they cannot win. One time they broke a window doing this, so we now put up netting and barricades as part of our homeland security. Cardinals are well known for attacking their reflections as well. While they are not powerful enough to break the glass, they do leave poop wherever they perch. That becomes a problem when they find a mirror on the side of a car. They perch on the front door and peck and poop away. One year that became such a problem that even a short visit to our house resulted in a car door and mirror covered in freshly produced fecal matter. We solved that problem by keeping old socks handy to put over the side mirrors of cars when guests arrived.

Once when I was home alone I heard a thump. I was busy writing and just ignored it. Then, a few minutes it happened again. I looked out the glass door to our lower patio and saw a crow on the grass at the far end of the patio. He was shuffling around like a drunk sailor. He soon got himself together and charged toward the door. He hit it hard and fell over. He got up and slowly made his way back to the grass. He went through the same process of shuffling and shaking himself and getting his legs in position for the charge. Then he did it again, and again. He then gave up and staggered out of site.

Benjamin Franklin felt the Turkey was a better symbol for our new nation than the Eagle. He thought the Bald Eagle was a bird of bad moral character, a lazy coward who prefers to steal food from other birds than fish himself, and easily chased away by much smaller birds. By contrast he thought the Turkey, though a bit vain and silly, was a much more respectable bird and one of courage who "would not hesitate to attack a Grenadier of the British Guard who should presume to invade his farm yard with a red coat on."

I had time to think about this as I watched the battle of the birds continue. I drew no conclusion as to which of the two species bests represented the characteristic of our nation. Perhaps we should consider other birds. How about considering fish, reptiles, amphibians or insects? Maybe we should hold a national contest. The Donkey and Elephant would have to be eliminated of course, but other than that there are so many possibilities.

Finally, the two gobblers got their heads separated. One popped out of the other like a cork from a bottle. They both fell over backwards and just rested there for a moment. Simultaneously, they got to their feet and staggered away in opposite directions. I'm certain there are lessons to be learned from this, but right now I can't think of any, and my head is beginning to hurt.

Oh Deer

It was a Saturday morning when our neighbor down over the hill called. Ron told me he had been hiking up in the woods on the hillside when he came across a doe stuck in a well that had been partially filled in. He said the deer was all curled up and unable to move. Its head was just below ground level. He wanted me to help him get it out, before the coyotes got to it. I said I would be happy to help and asked if he had a plan.

He said he had a fat rope. If I could get in under the deer's front legs and around its belly we might be able to pull it out. I was assigned that job because he recently had surgery on both knees and could not kneel. This sounded like as good a plan as any. I suggested I might bring the kids to see it. He suggested that I don't do that. He was bringing his shotgun, in case we could not get it out alive.

White Tailed deer are so abundant here that they are a problem. They eat our vegetables, young trees and lots of our ornamental plants. In the fall the bucks rub their antlers on our trees, stripping the bark and killing them. They collide with vehicles on the roads and highways, particularly in the fall rutting season, when the bucks are chasing the does. Some die from starvation in the winter. Since the wolf is gone from our area, the deer's main predator is the human.

We now allow our hilltop neighbor's son to hunt on our property. He parks his truck in front of our house and goes down into the woods. I tell him that when he goes down the deer come up and when he comes up the deer go down. I once got a photo of a large buck standing right by the tailgate of his truck while he was down over the hill. But he does manage to get deer quite often and shares his bounty with us. There is a certain satisfaction I get from eating the deer that ate our vegetables.

So, I met up with Ron at his house and we headed up the hillside. We came to the spot and, sure enough, there was a full-sized doe curled up in the well and unable to move. But that didn't stop her from trying. Instinctively, as we approached, she started thrashing around trying to flee. She managed to calm down just a little and I knelt down for a closer look. One side of her face was raw and bloody, probably from coyotes trying to get at her. She was obviously traumatized, and we had no idea if she had broken any legs. But she looked healthy and alert. When I knelt down to touch her, she thrashed around again.

Our dogs have a peculiar relationship with deer. We encourage the dogs to chase the deer away from our gardens and they do, sometimes. Once I saw a dog chase a large doe. They disappeared behind a spruce tree and then came running back into view again. But now the deer was chasing the dog. Once I woke early in the morning and looked out the window. Through a dreamy fog I saw the dogs out by the pond. They were lying in the grass and their heads were going back and forth in unison, as though they were watching a tennis match. The mist cleared enough for me to see the dogs were watching four deer running around in a circle, like the painted ponies on a carrousel.

Now, as I looked down at the deer in the well I tried to think of some point of reference from my past, some experience that I could draw on to help me in what I was about to do. I remember seeing Timmy trapped in a well once on TV. He was down very deep. Fortunately, he had his faithful dog, Lassie, to run and get help. And, unlike the poor creature below me, Timmy could grab onto the rope

I also seemed to recall Superman saving a kid from a well once, but he was Superman. The most recent experience I had with a rope and an animal in danger was when the cow appeared in the road by our house and I lassoed it. That was an experience I'd rather forget.

I took the end of the rope and tried to thread it behind the doe's front legs. She was totally freaked out now with eyes wide and muscles tense and quivering. I could smell her breath. It took several attempts, but finally I was able to lift her legs enough to get the rope behind them. I tried to get the rope centered on her belly but couldn't quite get there. I stood up and pulled the end of the rope to get it about as long as Ron's end with the deer in the middle. Now was the moment of truth.

We counted down from three and then pulled as hard as we could, Ron on one side of the hole and me on the other. The doe popped out of the hole like a cork from a bottle. Ron and I both fell over on our backs. We looked up and saw the deer thrashing about on the ground. She tried getting up a few times and finally succeeded. She tried to run and fell. I thought she had a broken leg and Ron would have to shoot her. But then she got up again and ran off into the woods.

So, we saved the deer and gave her a new lease on life. From time to time I saw her around our property. She was easy to identify with her scarred face. Perhaps someday, ironically, I thought she might show up on my dinner plate.

Aught Six Crops

All in all, it was a good year for crops in the Whitewater River valley. A wet spring did not hurt those farmers who were diligent or lucky enough to get planting done before the rains came, and came. Summer came reluctantly, but the corn was mostly more than knee high by the fourth of July.

Blueberries were the great proliferators at our home on the top of Lookout Road. We have nursed the few straggly plants for years, convincing them that they could thrive in clay soil, in spite of the evidence. We nestled them in pine needles and shredded oak leaves and energized them with liquid fertilizer to get them to a comfortable soil acidity level. We have been producing ripe fruit for several years, but this year was tops.

One of the nice aspects of the blueberries is that we don't (yet) worry about what to do with them all, unlike tomatoes and squash and even peaches some years. We just try to eat them all fresh. They began and ended my summer days – handfuls on cereal in the morning and on vanilla ice cream at night. Sometimes

Marty gets the "light" ice cream and I have to eat twice as much. I try to let the ice cream sit and soften a bit before I indulge. The texture is better that way and improved even more by whipping it a bit with my spoon which stirs in the berries. On the palate, the combination of tastes and texture is exquisite. Biting the berries releases bursts of new flavors and the feeling that, surely, I am getting close to nirvana.

Tomatoes, at some time during the planting, harvesting, processing and eating, make me think of Dad. He was a great lover of Jersey Beefsteaks. I remember the August vacation he somehow managed to afford when we rented a second-floor apartment in North Wildwood on the Jersey shore. This was a new experience for us. We never had family vacations. Mom and Dad were always too busy with jobs, raising seven kids, and too short of money. But by the time I finished sixth grade some of my siblings were working and no longer a financial burden. I think my older sisters actually convinced Mom and Dad to spend two weeks at the shore.

My younger sister, Kathy, and I spent most of the time running free, swimming, playing with water pistols, and getting sunburned. Dad seemed to spend much of his time sitting on the shaded porch and reading the paper. Late in the afternoon he would

196

open a beer and grab a huge tomato and a salt shaker. He would eat the whole tomato with great gusto, extolling its virtues and those of its lineage. Eating was one of his greatest pleasures and he was masterful at it. But I digress. Tomatoes have a way of making me do that.

We enjoy tomatoes right off the vine and, processed, right through the year. If you eat them fresh they should not be refrigerated because the skins get tough, so we eat lots before they go bad. We freeze many in plastic bags. Then, in winter, we can take them out, run them under hot water and the tough skins come right off. We then can use them in stews, soups and chili. This is much easier than the traditional canning method, though Marty does that also. This year the tomatoes were fairly plentiful, but not as well formed as we would have liked. There were not enough of the blistering hot days they like, strung along in a row. Gnarly tomatoes are not as good for freezing, so we did not freeze as many that way this year. So, Marty made salsa and canned it. I spent time cutting up tomatoes and juicing them – running them repeatedly through a hand-cranked contraption we have that separates the skins from the rest of the tomato. The juice was good fresh and we also froze some.

We had peaches again, from our one and only peach tree, which is an accident of birth. Family (Mullin clan) legend has it that Jim Mullin, my since deceased father-in-law, spit out a peach pit next to the compost heap near the barn many years ago and the tree sprouted. It was forgotten and did not begin to bear fruit till after Jim died. We have never sprayed it so it is susceptible to insects. Some years the raccoons and squirrels harvest it before we get to it. Some years it produces ripe fruit so heavy that the branches hang down close to the ground across the path I usually take with the tractor. It is both a menace and a delight.

Some years we freeze the peaches and some years we also dry the fruit. We slice them as thin as possible and place them on screens in the electric fruit and vegetable drier. We turn it on low and let the slices dry slowly for fourteen hours or better. The aroma fills the house. It is almost unbearably pleasant. The only scent that comes close is the lavender we grow and dry for use in closets, pouches and drawers. But we can eat the peaches.

Late summer brought national news of contaminated spinach and lettuce sold in groceries, reinforcing our conviction that the best and safest food is that which is grown locally on a small scale. We get meat from friends who organically raise livestock and

198

work as teachers. We grow veggies without the use of pesticides. If we contract some dreaded disease from our food at least we will know that it is our own doing. Our smugness may come back and bite us. So be it.

Now there is a decisive change in the air and frost has terminated all growth in the garden. I will wait till the earth surface is frozen enough for my boots to tread without sinking in the mud. Then I will go out early in the morning and pluck the garden plants up by the roots. I will then shred them along with the plentiful tree leaves for compost. Next spring there will come a day when warmth is in the air, and we will start all over again. Some day we will grow too old for all of this and will also be plucked from the earth. Till then we go about our business. Life is sweet. Life is bitter. The manure of memory nourishes the present. We begin where we ended and end where we began. But I digress. Aging does that to me.

Passings

Our min-van is gone. Purchased new in 1995, it
got us through a lot of personal history. It was often
filled with kids going to events. It transported our kids
back and forth to summer camps and then to college,
laden down with all their furniture (mostly precious
junk) and possessions, resembling a dust bowl scene
from The Grapes of Wrath. It took us far off on trips
with friends to go bicycling or birding and visiting
friends and family all over the country.

We bought it before it was un-cool to own such
a vehicle. It apparently became a symbol of something
young people detest, a symbol of settling down and
growing old. We tend to prefer practicality over status
when making such a major purchase, so its loss of
appeal to others meant nothing to us. It had over
123,000 miles on it and we decided its time had come.

Many years ago, my brother Danny took his
meager inheritance from our parents and bought the
biggest motorcycle he could find. Shortly thereafter he
crashed the thing. Both he and it survived, but
recovery was much more difficult for him. I went to
see him in the hospital. He was in pain, on medication,
and rambled on and on about various things. Eventually
he got to the topic of the motorcycle. Much to my

relief, he was determined to get rid of it. "Tommy," he said, "sometimes you just have to be able to give things up."

This past week my laptop computer had a stroke and is in intensive care. I have confidence in our computer doctor because I don't understand a word he says. If anyone can save it, he can. Have you ever tried to administer CPR through a USB port? Take my word for it, it does not work. This is my work computer and traveling office. It introduced me to a wealthy African widow whose husband was assassinated by some bloody dictator and needed my help to transfer a large sum of money to my account. In spite of her personal tragedy, she was kind enough to offer me a large cut of the loot. I was tempted to help her, but I was afraid that the foreign money wouldn't work in the machine at our local car wash, most of the time it won't even take our money.

Sometimes my laptop got too personal. It once sent me an email asking if I was horny, then one asking if I wanted to attract men with bigger breasts. I didn't know which way to take that. There may be guys who are attracted to men with big breasts, but not me. Sometimes my laptop made me angry. Sometimes it made me blush. I can't make it angry. I can't make it blush.

While it's in the ICU, I'm using an ancient laptop. It has an old version of Windows, Windows BC. It has a manual transmission and I have to use the clutch peddle to get from one program to another.

Much as I'm dependent on computers, I long ago realized that technology is not the path to salvation. I think I first realized this when I had my first computer malfunction. I called in a technician and I thought he would fix it. He looked at it and said "Huh!" This is not something I want to hear from my plumber, physician, or tech guy.

The new car now sits in the garage in the same place the old min-van sat. I resent this. I think it would have been better to park it outside for a few days, and gradually put it in the garage, for a few hours at first, then a day. I think that would have been more respectful.

Of Man and Bird

The northern shrike is a harmless looking song bird about the size of a robin. It catches insects, rodents and other birds and impales them on thorns and barbwire. Sometimes its prey is as big and heavy as the shrike itself.

Brad cuts people open with a knife. His is the surgeon who fixed my hernia. The shrike comes back and eats its prey. Brad sewed me up and went off to the Super Bowl.

They following weekend I stood on the causeway at the north end of the lake and saw the shrike, a rare visitor to our parts. It was our first sighting of the bird in the wild. The morning was cold and the air was brisk. The five of us – Marty, me, friends June and Walt, and Marty's sister, Beth, visiting from Tennessee – stood and chatted, looking out at the lake. The sun shone brightly, trying but failing to provide much warmth.

I visited Brad a few times before the operation and found him to be a likable character, friendly and optimistic. The kind of guy I'd like to sit with and have a beer. We talked and joked just before he went to scrub up and, I suppose, sharpen his knives. Then the anesthesiologist came in and told me that I might die from a heart attack or various other things. I think his point was that it would not be his fault.

I'm just happy that Brad and the Shrike are two separate species and follow much different post-incision protocols.

Dear Grandson,

You know I love you right? I want you to be successful at whatever you do, and I want to support your endeavors and activities as best I can, but sometimes this is not easy for me. The last time I visited you, for example, I was more than happy to help you feed your cows when you asked me to. But you fed them rice and milk and cheese. I can't help but think there is something very wrong about feeding dairy products to cows. This seems to me to be just short of feeding them hamburger, and I could never go there. The rice? Maybe, but then you cooked it and fed it to them from a bowl with a spoon. I just don't understand that. And why did we have to wear fire fighter hats when we did this? The cows seemed okay with this, so I didn't say anything at the time.

Then, when we were riding the train on the couch in your den, and you asked, no insisted, that I be the engineer, I did the best I could. I understood that there was a cow on the tracks near Oshkosh, and why I had to pull the brake as hard and fast as I could, and why we had to get off the train and chase the cow off the tracks. But I had trouble understanding how there could be an elephant on the tracks on the way to Kalamazoo, and a giraffe on the tracks on the way to

Cucamonga. Did they escape from zoos perhaps? If so, it would have been helpful if you had explained that to me at the time. But I was so happy that we got through that trip without killing any animals or endangering any passengers.

Then there was the time in your playroom when you were a captain on a ship sailing the ocean and you wanted me to be a penguin. A penguin? I was totally unprepared for that. I tried my best, but I felt so inadequate. To your credit, you tolerated my bumbling performance gracefully, but I felt that I let you down. Can you understand how hard it is to be a penguin? I could do a really great lion or puppy dog. But, as you so helpfully pointed out, that would be silly. What would a lion or puppy dog be doing in the middle of the ocean?

So, I went home and I read about penguins, and I watched them carefully on YouTube videos, copying their every move. I practiced and practiced and finally got in touch with my inner penguin. But the next time I visited you were not a ship's captain anymore. You were floating down a river on a raft and you wanted me to be a beaver, a beaver of all things. Do you have any idea how hard it is to be a beaver? I think it would take years and years for even the most accomplished actor to master that part. So, I'm so sorry if I let you down on that one. But once again, you didn't seem to mind.

I don't mean to complain, and it's not just that I was angry because you got so many more toys for Christmas than I did. I think the total count was something like two hundred twenty-seven to zero. But I'm over that now, and it was very nice of you to let me play with SOME of them. Actually, if you count the little ones in your Christmas stocking I think it was like two hundred thirty-three to zero, but like I say, that's all in the past.

It's not you, it's me. It really is. You see I am as old as dirt and stuck in my version of reality. I find it hard at times to even think outside the box, let alone crawl out of the box like an alligator as you would probably want me to do. You are not yet three years old and you don't even seem to see any boxes. If you did see one it would not be a box at all but a car, or a truck, or an ambulance, or a fire engine.

But now it is a new year and I resolve to do better. I will try my best to do what you want and be what you want me to be. I really will, even before I get my coffee in the morning, which is often the case. I'll sing along about the five little monkeys jumping on the bed as many times as you wish. I won't even ask about what happened to them after they fell off the bed, and I'll always remember, I promise, to clap my hands and give you an m&m when you poop in the potty.

Happy New Year!

Sincerely,

Poppy

Musical Musing

While at Redondo Beach in Southern California recently, I had the pleasure of attending a concert of the Hollywood String Quartet, performing works by Beethoven and Schumann. I sat next to a little, old woman who, before the concert started, was a lively and delightful chatterbox. I think she said she was 85 years old. By the second movement of the first piece she was fast asleep. I so admired how she did this, simply, slowly dropping her head down and closing her eyes, without bringing any attention to herself at all. At first glance you might think that she was just focusing intently on the intricate interplay of cello, violin and viola. Maybe, on some level of unconsciousness she was, but she was definitely sleeping.

Then the old man sitting directly in front of me began to nod off, repeatedly dropping his head and then jerking it back upright. He was tallish, and did not have the same center of gravity as the little, round woman next to me. So, as his head dropped he started leaning forward and to his left. He did this several times, each time lasted a little longer and he leaned a bit farther towards the woman next to him. I thought he might keel over onto her lap. Apparently, so did she, judging from the worried look on her face, not at all appreciating the violation of her personal space by this stranger. I thought about kicking the back of his chair, but I don't like to interfere with nature unless really necessary.

My eye lids started getting heavy, and my mind drifted off, back in time and across the continent, from sea to shining sea. I was sitting and enjoying a cold beer with my buddy George in a tavern on the Jersey shore. It was early in the 1970's. We were captivated by two lovely, young women who were playing guitars and singing sweet songs of the period, in perfect harmony. The crowd was noisy and paying little attention to them, but George and I certainly were. When they finished their first set, we chatted with them. When George mentioned that he and I play

208

guitar they insisted that we play a few numbers while they took their break, and so we did.

I got the twelve-string guitar, six more strings than were needed as far as I was concerned, and I didn't know quite what to do with them. I decided to ignore the extra ones and hope they would go away. George is a big guy, with a big voice. He launched into a raucous number from our vast repertoire of raucous songs. I followed along, trying to prevent my fingers from getting tangled in the extra strings, and singing it a way that could be appreciated as harmony if you were drunk enough, and most were. We may not have been very good, but we were loud. We were two coyotes howling at the moon.

We got everyone's attention and they liked us. They actually liked us. Our biggest fan was a guy on a barstool who yelped and clapped and called for more. We obliged. During our second raucous number he started singing along, as though he knew the song, but his mouth did not deliver actual words. What came out was a garbled mess, sort of like singing in tongues. But he was having a great time. Just when we came to the end of the song, his lights went out and he fell over with a thud. He was out cold.

Only those close to him seemed to notice, but George and I wasted no time. We swung into action immediately, returning the instruments to their rightful owners and high-tailing it out of there. As we drove away I was concerned. According to the conventional wisdom of the day, drunks tend to be somewhat immune to fall injuries. Inebriation relaxes all the muscles. They don't brace themselves while falling. They just go with the flow and fall gracefully. In spite of this seemingly valid scientific rationale, I worried. He certainly did not fall gracefully. He tipped over like a tin soldier, taking the bar stool with him. I don't think he ever left his seat.

What if he had a stroke or hit his head and died when he fell. Could we be held responsible? Investigators could easily lift our fingerprints from the guitars and there were plenty of witnesses. Some of them may even be able to remember where they were that night the morning after. But what could they possibly charge us with? Musical manslaughter?

I looked around at the concert audience. Well over half of those in attendance were over 65 years of age, me included. I thought that many of us were ready for nice nap. I hoped that the musicians would take it as a complement if we dozed off. What better

210

purpose could music serve than to provide peaceful, blissful slumber?

The man in front of me was now on the very verge of toppling. I was able to catch his full profile. I was struck by how much he looked like that face on the barroom floor, many years ago, many years older. Could it be? No, no, I was just getting drowsy and imagining things.

TSA Tale

Wife, Marty, and I were just starting back home from a trip to visit her aunt in Southern California. We were on a crowded shuttle bus from the rental car return company to our terminal at LAX. I decided to get ahead of the game and get out my driver's license to put in my shirt pocket, to have available to get through security. I pulled out my wallet and flipped it open, only to find that my driver's license was not there, where it was supposed to be.

I looked everywhere in the wallet, then I began a frantic search through my pockets, my over-stuffed backpack and shoulder bag. I did this again and again, keenly aware that I was being seen by all the hip passengers as a neurotic geezer. I didn't care. I had to

211

find it. I could not get through security without a photo ID. I told Marty, sitting across from me. She asked for my wallet. I gave it to her. She went through it and gave it back.

We got to the terminal (aptly named), and found a seat in the busy, crowded concourse. We emptied my bags, dirty laundry and all. We went through every pocket, every nook and cranny. Then we did it again. When had I last seen it? I flashed back to our departure from Cincinnati, when I used it to get through security on our way out, then to get the rental car. Had I seen it since then?

I had no other photo ID. But wait. I did. I had a copy of a book I wrote. It had a photo of me on the back cover. I recalled reading about popular author, Bill Bryson, who was in a similar situation and used his book photo to get through customs when returning from the UK to the US. But that was long before 9-11, and he went through quite an ordeal. But I had no other option.

I whipped out my book and walked up to two TSA agents who were sitting at a table, chatting idly. I explained my situation and showed them my book. They were amused and impressed. They look at the book and then back at me. They wrote down the name

212

of the book and asked me about it. One of them read my name from the cover and repeated it: "Tom Cooney, Tom Cooney," as if trying to recall, "Should I know you?"

Perhaps she was confusing me with Tom Clancy, or Michael Clooney. I wanted to say "Yes, yes, I am a famous author and celebrity. I have been on numerous talk shows and am in negotiations with Spielberg's people for a major motion picture based on my book. I will give you an autographed copy of my book if you will just, kindly permit me to pass through to my flight." But lying to a federal agent would surely be a major offence. Attempted bribery would undoubtedly add several years to my sentence.

They said I would have to go to the security line and present my case to the grim-faced women who was the gatekeeper, the decider of who shall pass. I did so, and once again presenting my case, I got a smile, an actual smile. She never looked at me, focusing all the time on her computer screen, but I could clearly see the gleam of the braces in the back of her mouth as she broke into a grin, perhaps for the first time all day.

She made a slight motion and another agent appeared—presumably a supervisor. She did look at me, rather intensely, as I repeated my story yet again.

She held up the book next to my face and said "Yes, that definitely is you". She said she would let me pass, but I would have to go through another procedure.

Yes! I was ready to do whatever it took. I would happily strip naked and bend over, allowing them to probe my butt for explosives. I would promise not to pass gas, as long as they did not pull my finger. I was ushered off to my own, private security guy who stuck to me like glue as he directed me through the process. He patted me down thoroughly, and then he went through my bags, thoroughly, very thoroughly, dirty laundry and all.

I passed. I passed and was on my way. On the long flight back, I worried about what I would have to go through to get a replacement for my driver's license. I got home and, as I was unpacking my bags, my driver's licenses fell out on to the floor.

I learned three things from this:

1. If you plan to fly, you should write a book and put your picture on the back of it. Carry a copy with you. You never know when you might need it.
2. If something important wants to get lost, it will. There is nothing you can do about it, even with

the help of federal agents. You will never find
it until it is ready to be found.
3. ALWAYS KEEP YOUR DRIVER'S LICENSE IN YOUR
WALLET WHERE IT BELONGS!

Silver Alert!

"An endangered person is missing from the City of
Lawrence, Marion County, Indiana"

I keep getting such messages on my phone since
I signed on for emergency alerts. I get weather alerts
and road closing alerts. I didn't realize I'd be getting
Amber alerts for missing kids and Silver alerts for old
farts like me. The missives give the names of the poor
old geezers, a photo and a description of what they
were wearing and where they were last seen. Usually I
later get another ding on my phone and find out that
the alert has been cancelled and Trudy Portman is
safely back in the nursing home. I don't know Trudy
but I am truly happy that she is safe. Now that I think
of it I don't think I ever got an alert cancellation on
Millard Hackenbush.   I wonder what happened to him.

Maybe Siri would know, but we are not on
speaking terms right now. We had another
disagreement over some directions. I got angry and

said some things I should not have. The breaking point came when there was this long silence and she asked me if I was still there. I said I was recalculating. I shouldn't have said that but I had no idea she could pick up on sarcasm.

Someday I will get that crisp ding on my phone and find that the alert is for me. That could happen any day now. What do I do then? Hopefully it will tell me where I was last seen before I vanished, abducted by space aliens perhaps. Something has to explain why I have no idea where I am and how I got here. I think I will just somehow find my way back to where I was last seen and wait to be found.

I'm thinking I should start an official old farts club. To be a member you must be over 65 and be proud of your advanced years. This club does not go for euphemisms. We are not seniors, elderly or chronologically challenged. If you are uncomfortable calling us old farts we will settle for geezer. You pay an annual membership fee and get a genuine membership card entitling you to all the rights and privileges. Big discounts may apply at retail stores, gas stations, theaters and restaurants. You may get reduced airfare and better access to public services. To find out you must tell the clerk (or whoever) that you are an Old Fart, loudly and boldly.

I've been married for 138 years (give or take a hundred) and you would think that by now my wife and I would understand each other perfectly. Yet there are moments when she speaks to me and I have no idea what she is saying. I recognize all the words she says and know their Standard English usage, but they are in an order and sequence that I cannot make any sense of. Clearly, she wants a response, some decision or agreement perhaps. Sometimes I can identify the topic or issue, but sometimes I can't even do that. When I reply, it is like we are suddenly using totally different languages, ironically consisting of the same words. It is amazing. It becomes a total quagmire, a maze of sentences. It can be very difficult finding my way out. I wish I had an app for this so I could just punch a few spots on my phone with my thumbs and we could communicate effectively again.

I do hope such an app is developed before I get that Silver Alert on me. Assuming I get found, my wife will want to know what happened. I doubt that I will be able to explain what happened, but I might be able to explain why I was wearing madras shorts and a Hawaiian shirt in the dead of winter. Perhaps Siri and I will be on speaking terms again and she will come to my defense. It could happen. You have to think positively when you get old.

Buckeye Encounter

I was working on some fence posts out by the mail box when a guy driving a car with Ohio plates pulled up and rolled down his window. He looked bewildered. He said his GPS must be wrong, "Is this an actual road?' he asked.

I just had to laugh, but having grown up a city boy, I could relate to his predicament. We are on top of a hill. He had already gotten lost on our one lane road that is about forty percent pot hole and was, as far as he could tell, about to drop down into an abyss.

I assured him that this was indeed a road, and gave him directions back to civilization. Then he asked me what he should do if he encountered another vehicle coming up the road. I told him he should hope that it wasn't another Buckeye.

Oh, the simple joys of country living.

Epilogue

I got as far as I could with the puzzle and it was still far from completion. Many pieces are still missing and I had some left that didn't seem to fit anywhere. I had been so caught up in the past that I lost all sense of time. I was exhausted but felt compelled to go on and make another trip to the attic to find more pieces.

I climbed the ladder, this time with a flashlight in hand. I returned to the corner and searched through the pile again. I could find no more pieces. I thought they had to be there somewhere. I searched again, on my hands and knees, without any success. I spread the search outward from the corner looking through boxes and meticulously checking every inch of the floor. I covered the entire attic but could find no other pieces. I was up there for hours.

Dejected and very weary, I climbed back down. I went back to the den and could not believe what I saw, or more precisely, what I did not see. After all the strangeness I had experienced, this was the strangest of all. There was nothing on the top of the card table. The puzzle and the box were gone.

Now, some things entirely different

(Fiction and such)

The following are some strange pieces I found in the attic that don't seem to fit anywhere in the puzzle or in my life experiences.

Omer and the Spider

Once upon a time there was a very big spider who decided to make a web in one of the open ends of an old covered bridge. Now this was a rather ambitious endeavor, even for such a large spider, considering the size of the opening, but he had lots of time. The bridge was not used much anymore; having fallen to decay, neglect, and the weight of time. It was old and tired and sagging in the middle but had served the people well. It now had a weight limit and would soon be closed. A few miles down the river stood the new bridge, opened just the month before. The old bridge was mainly used by locals as a shortcut to town.

The spider worked very diligently, even by spider standards and got the web completed by sunrise on a pleasant fall morning. Wet with dew drops, each thread of the intricate silk tapestry glistened in the morning light.

Omer Prickle was working construction, on a job that needed to get under roof before winter. He was late again, and was driving fast, slowing just enough to navigate the approach to the bridge without too much of a jarring bounce. He never saw the web, but for the spider it was quite a shock. His whole world was suddenly ripped apart and he found himself being tossed about in the air. He came to rest dangling upside-down from a single remaining thread attached to the roof. Instinctively he righted himself, looked around, and saw that his entire creation was gone.

Not being one to brood over such events, the spider went right back to building the web again. He was about halfway down from the top, attempting to span the opening vertically, when Edna Hopple came rocketing down the road. She was on her way to deliver the cookies she made for the baked goods sale at the Amvets.

Edna was 85 years of age at the time and behind the wheel of the old Buick she and her dearly departed husband, Lester, bought brand new some 19 years earlier. Those that knew her well said that she should not be driving anymore at all and the spider would probably have agreed if anyone had bothered to ask him. She was nearly blind and could barely see above the dashboard, even sitting on the fat Sears & Roebuck catalogue she used as a booster seat.

Her driving skills were really not an issue in this situation though. Hardly anyone driving down the road and approaching the bridge would see the spider, and it is highly unlikely that anyone seeing it would stop. This time the spider ended up spinning and swinging on the long thread. So, then he had to start all over again. Then he had Omer and Edna going home, and a few in between.

Myrtle Duffle went to visit her mother-in-law at the nursing home. Then there were the two guys from the city driving the Sears delivery truck. They got lost and pulled over by the bridge to check their map. This was long before the days of GPS navigational systems, and they were taking a new refrigerator to Mort Markel's place, which was way off the beaten track. Mort's wife, Bertha, tried to give them directions on the phone but they wouldn't listen. "If'n they think they can find us with just a street address they is badly mistaken," she warned, and she was right.

Each one ripped through that web without any awareness of the damage they did, to it and to the poor spider's psyche, not that they would have cared much if they knew. But to the spider this was major, a life changing trauma. But all he knew to do was to start knitting his web again, and he stayed up all night, producing the most incredible web. It may have had more threads per inch than any spider web that came before. It was so big and thick that it would surely be seen from quite a distance and withstand great impact.

Omer was in a hurry to get to work that morning, having been warned the day before that he would be fired if he showed up late one more time. He headed out of his place half-awake before the sun was up. It was dark and foggy when he got near the bridge. He was within about 70 yards of the opening when his engine died. He got out of his old, beat-up pick-up truck and did about what one would expect from Omer. He kicked the truck and began cussing up a storm. He knew the problem all too well, since this was not the first time it happened. He had run out of gas. Ever since his fuel gage died, he had no way of telling when this might happen, and often over estimated how far he could go on a couple gallons.

He rummaged around in the back of his truck, came up with a gas can, and began trudging up the road towards the bridge as fast as he could walk. The closest filling station was just a mile or so on the other side. If he hurried he just might be able to make it back and get to the construction site on time. He left home extra early to be extra safe time-wise, just in case of such a misfortune, having been subject to several recently.

Not being in the best of shape, Omer was about out of breath and slowing considerably as he climbed the approach to the bridge. There were no witnesses to what happened next except the spider, and Sheriff Johnson struggled to come up with a chronology that made sense for his report.

Edna was headed back to the Amvets to help with the clean-up from the big event the day before. The first rays of the morning sun were just starting to burn off the fog, but not nearly enough yet that she could see what it was she hit as she entered the opening of the bridge. Whatever it was, it was big and made quite a thump on the hood of her big old sedan and stuck on it. Her first thought was that it was a deer, but it was so dark in the bridge that she couldn't tell for sure. She stopped but didn't want to get out of the car. She started up again, slowly at first. The car seemed to be running fine.

When she got off the bridge at the other end, she could see a bit better. It did not look like a deer at all. It looked more like something wrapped in a cocoon of sorts and stuck to her hood. Whatever it was, she did not want to mess with it. She decided to just drive it in to Al's service station and let him look at it. She stepped on the gas and away she went.

Somehow, she made it. Al couldn't believe what he was seeing. It looked like a man holding something and covered with sticky gauze. The gauze was so thick that he could not make out the man's features. He called the sheriff and got his deputy, Jared Brandenburger. Al didn't try to explain on the phone. He just told Jared he better get over to the garage fast and bring the EMS, and then he hung up the phone.

The paramedic, Sam Brundle, uncovered the thing enough to see that it was Omer and that he was holding a gas can. He was alive, and rushed to the nearest hospital, Foghorn Memorial, over in Jefferson County.

Sheriff Johnson and Jared tried to interview Edna, but she made no sense at all. She just kept babbling something about giant spiders destroying the county, and later, had to be treated for shock. The scene of the crime yielded little evidence. They found Omer's truck and figured out he was walking for gas. They examined the bridge and found nothing unusual. If they had looked under the bridge they would have found a mighty big spider.

Omer eventually recovered from an assortment of broken bones, but had no recollection of the event at all, though some folks said he just didn't want to talk about it. Edna never did recover from the shock. Her children insisted that she never drive again and she never did. Both Omer and Edna had a severe case of arachnophobia. Edna ended up in a nursing home where she spent her remaining days roaming the halls and mumbling about spiders and insects.

The story got passed around as such stories do, at the Quick and Easy filling station and bait store, at Sally's café where the ROMEOs (Retired Old Men Eating Out) gathered at the liars table in the morning, at Olga's Hairum amid the rustle of old magazines and the hum of hair dryers, at Bart's Bar over shots and beers. Several years have gone by but the story is still likely to come up from time to time for review and discussion. The years have added many speculations and theories.

Kids around camp fires still shake in terror at the thought of the giant spider out there in the night, plotting revenge. Some say Omer, living all alone in his trailer out in the woods, wraps himself head to toe in fine silk threads each night before he goes to bed. He is seldom seen in town anymore and avoids conversation. It was a sign of courage for a child to take the dare and creep out to look in his window on Halloween night.

He put a stop to that when he got his dog, Demon. He still has the old truck but it is mostly a source of frustration trying to keep it running. He spends lots of time under it covered in grease, scraping his knuckles and cussing up a storm, but he keeps the tank full of gas.

Edna's car went to her great grandson, Bobby, who enjoys being under it a lot. He spends as much time working on it as he can. When he graduates from high school he plans to get a job as a mechanic and open up a garage of his own someday. The car still has the dent in the hood and Bobby intends to leave it alone. He thinks that the story of how it got there may fascinate the girls and make them want to curl up in his lap.

Mort and Bertha got their refrigerator and it still works fine. We assume the two Sears delivery guys made it back to the city, but they were not heard from again.

The bridge closed and became an eyesore and the county planned to take it down when the money could be found. Then some kids playing hooky accidentally set it on fire. It started right in the middle, burned in both directions, then the bridge collapsed into the river. The water put out the fire, except for the brush on both sides that took quite a while to control. Then the floods came and took the remaining beams way down river, including the one the spider dangled from. It is half buried in the bank, almost a mile away. When the water is low, Bobby stands on it to fish and has no understanding of its significance. When the water is high it is a favorite place for trout.

The day would come when folks would yearn for the old covered bridges and the lifestyle they represented, but not back then. Many would lament the death of common childhood structures and artifacts, and organize to preserve and restore them, but not back then. Then and now are as different as night and day in many ways but not in others. We laugh, we cry, we mourn the same, but no one mourns for the spider.

Memory of Marcus

The rain started gently enough, giving no indication of what was to come. Marcus said we should wait it out as we sat in our boat in the middle of a large and unfamiliar lake. If it got bad we could make a dash for the nearest cove, run the boat ashore and head up through the woods for cover.

I tried to picture that in my mind as I hunkered down under my rain coat and watched the surface of the lake come alive with ripples. I had no idea where we were or how far a walk it would be to the nearest road or shelter. Neither did Marcus for that matter, though he would never admit it. He was that kind of guy, always darting ahead like a tadpole, staying one stroke in front of me and just out of reach. I don't know why it was so irresistible for me to follow. He led me to places I would never have gone, mentally and physically.

The lake was full of lore and wonder, pristine and alluring. He promised a memorable, perhaps life changing experience. Free from phones and the ability to be connected to the world of humans, we would become fully submerged in nature, then return to our normal lives with a new understanding and sense of purpose. Either that or the experience might kill us. He didn't mention that.

He had it all figured out, the spot where we would slip our borrowed row boat into the remote lake. We would live as simply as possible; fishing, hiking, exploring. He was a city boy with very little experience in these things. His confidence often outran his abilities. I watched him now, two days out, staring out over the water, jaw and mind set.

The first bolt of lightning came suddenly, followed too closely by hostile thunder that rattled the boat. His eyes flashed as he grabbed the oars with his huge hands and pulled powerfully, leaning way back to get full advantage with each stroke. He headed for the nearest shore, some hundred yards away. The storm rolled in low, following us across the water. The rain was now a deluge and I feared the boat would fill with water before we made shore. He was facing me, rowing backwards. There was nothing I could do but try to guide him. Facing ahead, I had the better view of the coast that too slowly grew in size as we approached.

We were wet, completely wet, except for the trunk of our bodies that were covered by our rain coats. He was as scared as I was. I could see it in his eyes. I can't recall ever seeing him this way before. Marcus was always confident and in command. His physical strength was matched by his mental agility. He had a curiosity about so many things, from the philosophical to the mundane. He wanted to know how things worked and why things were the way they were. He latched on to a topic like a shark and tore it apart until, totally satiated, he moved on to the next. Now his eyes were wide and wild looking above his high cheek bones, like a cornered lion. His long mane and beard dripped as the rain pelted his drooping hat.

Lightning and thunder crashed ferociously all around us. The wind was strong but it helped push us to the shore. I pointed to a clear spot that looked like a slope we could easily climb. Marcus hit it dead on, but it was all mud and much steeper than it looked from a distance. The water was choppy now and wind stronger. It pushed the boat around so I was now facing backwards. The water here was too shallow for the oars and we drifted just past the muddy bank where a low overhanging limb nearly took off my head. I didn't see it till Marcus yelled for me to duck, which I did as I turned to see it. Marcus grabbed onto it and then I grabbed some brush and we pulled the boat tightly to shore. We managed to get out gracelessly, slipping and sliding in mud, and tie the boat to a tree. We huddled under the trees and watched the boat, with all our provisions, filling with water.

The day that had started so pleasantly was now in shambles. We were wet and chilled to the bone. But the storm passed over and the sun came out, and just before setting, stretched a rainbow across the sky.

We managed to retrieve our gear, strip and get into some relatively dry clothing we had wrapped in plastic bags. We stretched rope between two dripping trees, hanging things to dry. Then came the sunset and with it a swarm of mosquitoes, attacking every inch of exposed skin and even trying to bite through our clothing. We dosed ourselves with repellent, which kept them at bay just inches away.

Angry lake, bellicose sky, all behind us for now. The lake and sky were tranquil. But what was to come? Our car was across the lake somewhere far away. We had no plan. We were just relieved to be off the water. We pitched our tent and crawled inside, after eating whatever we could salvage from cans and floating plastic bags of leftover scraps.

We went about trying to methodically kill each mosquito in the tent so we could get some sleep free of the buzzing in our ears. Then, just as we began to doze, there would be another buzz. One or both of us would suddenly awake and seek out the creature for destruction. Neither one of us could sleep as long as there was the slightest buzz. This went on and on throughout the night. When exhaustion brought slumber, I dreamt I was hearing mosquitos, getting up and going after them. There was no longer any distinction between my dreams and my awake state. I've never had such an experience before or since that bizarre night.

Daylight came with exquisite brightness as the sun attempted to burn the wetness from the land and water. All the world in front of us was shrouded in mist as deep and thick as porridge. With great effort, we managed to turn over and drain the boat. We packed our things and I insisted on taking a turn at the oars. We pushed off from the shore. We could not see where we were going. I could barely see Marcus and the other end of the boat.

I rowed hard at first and then slowed to a steady pace, not knowing if we were going straight or in circles. We had no reference point except the dew at the end of our noses. This seemed to go on for hours, but at this point we had lost all concept of time. We were sharing an experience that, aided by lack of sleep, was almost hallucinogenic. I finally stopped rowing. We sat and stared at the magical mist. Taking in the smells and the sounds of the lake, the lapping water, the distant birds, the croaking frogs.

We looked at each other deeply and suddenly experienced a total release of all tension as we drifted without concern. We started laughing and could not stop, rocking the boat to the point that we had to get hold of ourselves for fear of tipping over. That made us start laughing even harder. The storm of laughter played itself out and, as we drifted contentedly, the mist began to lift. We could see the distant shore again. Reluctantly, we made our way back to safety.

I don't know why this all came back to me so vividly just now, thirty years later, standing in my vegetable garden. I haven't seen Marcus in over twenty years. I hear from him from time to time. He is settled now and so am I, far away from each other. Back then we were young and eager, looking for adventure and trying to figure out the world and our places in it.

New Bird Discovered at Brookville Lake

Ornithologist Jack Peters is astounded as he peers through his microscope. The DNA evidence is clear. But how could this be? How everyone in the birding community, professionals and amateurs alike could have missed this strange new bird for so long, is hard to comprehend.

A relative of the woodpecker, the Cooney pecker-pecker, is an avian of peculiar appetite, a man-eater and a menace. The bird does exactly as it says, emitting a harsh call that sounds like "pecker, pecker", before fiercely attacking the most delicate part of unsuspecting bathers and boaters.

Feasting only on live male humans, the birds finish quickly with the genital appetizer and work their way through the entire body. Sometimes they will discard the brain, seemingly viewing it as the most useless part of the male anatomy.

The bird was first discovered by amateur birder Tom Cooney, who caught an attack on video and put it on YouTube. It was an instant hit. Now the beautiful lake in rural southeast Indiana is under siege by hordes of scientist from all over the world.

What they have learned so far is that there are two kinds of pecker-peckers, the German and the Irish. While sharing the same appetites, their methods of attack are very different. The German pecker-peckers form large flocks that dive-bomb from high above, quickly and without warning. The victim is gone within minutes. The Irish pecker-pecker flies gently down and lands on the victim's shoulder. He then begins to whisper in the ear, going on and on about the fairies and the leprechauns, the shades of green in the Emerald Isle, and the pot of gold at the end of the rainbow. The victim soon falls fast asleep, the bird's clan members arrive, and leisurely feast for hours while dancing and singing.

Henrietta Robin, senior researcher for the World Ornithological Council, warns against panic. "The more we know of the bird the less we are concerned," she says. "There have been only a few deaths reported and it only eats live males." Many men on the lake don't move much and are mistaken for dead, so the birds stay away from them. Alcohol is a strong deterrent. In fact, Dr. Peters recommends that all males on the lake stay as still as they can and drink lots of alcoholic beverages. Your life may depend on it. She also believes that the birds will soon tire of such a bland diet and develop more sophisticated tastes, such as dead possums and other road kill. "Then," she says, "they may be even more useful to us than they are now."

Beard Tips

When our town celebrated its one-hundredth birthday, men were encouraged to grow beards and enter a beard contest. Having had a beard for about thirty-five years of my life, I had some advice to offer. Growing a beard can be a fun and healthy activity and can lead to great prosperity and success in life, but don't count on it. But if you are going to do it, you should do it right.

When your beard first starts to come in it is important to fertilize it. Treat it like any other crop. Spread it with copious amounts of manure, working it into your skin with your fingers. Do this at least once a week for several weeks and let it settle in for a day or two before washing away the excess.

When it begins to look like a real beard you should treat it with pesticide and herbicides. Anything you might use on your field or garden will work on your chin. Round Up is good and relatively safe for the environment. Atrazine, commonly used on corn, works well. Studies show that small amounts of it can turn otherwise healthy male frogs into hermaphrodites, but so what. There are risks with everything. Just think of all the risks our forefathers took when they settled the town. Besides, worse things could happen to you.

If you have already started your beard you may notice that children are particularly attracted to bearded men around Christmas time. They may want to hop on your lap and ask you for all kinds of things. Given the way things are today, I strongly advise you to be very careful about this.

Don't be afraid of what you will look like or what people will say. Growing a beard is a virile pursuit. With few exceptions, only men can do it. When the bicentennial is over, keep that beard. When people ask me why I grow a beard I tell them that is the wrong question. It grows there naturally. No one asks me why I grow hair on my head. In fact, if I shaved my head people would probably ask me why I shaved it. The right question is: Why would you want to take a very sharp and dangerous piece of metal and scrape your face with it?

Enjoy the Bicentennial and grow that beard.

Boomer Mania

After a brutal winter, scientist warn, even the slightest hint of warm weather can trigger a strong and potentially dangerous physiological response in humans. Symptoms include rapid mood swings, the shedding of clothing, digging in dirt, and overexertion in the outdoors.

"As a result we are likely to see high demand on urgent care centers, emergency rooms and cardiac care units," says Doctor Sun Rizes, Dean of the School of Seasonal Disorders at MIT. "Most of the demand will come from aging baby boomers," he continues. "We have isolated a chemical in the brain directly responsible for delusional thinking and uncontrollable physical urges. While it is present at all ages, it increases as we age and is triggered exponentially upon retirement."

Most years this is referred to as spring fever. But after a particularly long and cold winter it is likely to be more of a dangerous mania of epidemic proportions as it spreads.

Tales of Joseph

It was a beautiful fall day when the strange events began that would change my life forever. I was hiking along the trails on our 35 acres of hilltop property in Southeast Indiana. I still say "our" from habit, though since the tragic death of my wife it is now "my" land.

She was supposed to live much longer than I, coming from a long line of women who lived well into their nineties. Then a truck crossed the center line on a winding stretch of county highway and met her car head on. That happened eight months ago. I retired soon after that, and spend my time tending to the property, volunteering in the local community and thinking about the life we had together. Belinda and I had been married for thirty-five years when the accident happened. We raised two children who are now off on their own and far away. I am still struggling to get over the loss of my wife as I make the transition from Dr. Patrick Malory, psychotherapist to Pat Malory, country gentleman. I spend a lot of time reflecting, perhaps too much.

I started out to walk the east trail through the woods, winding down off the top of the hill. I was joined by our two trusty mutts, Jasper and Tulip. Since the kids were little we always picked up strays or they picked up us. I think that those who wanted to get rid of a dog would drive around in the country, looking for a home with a swing set and toss the animal out, realizing that any home with small children would be likely to take it in. We always did, the kids promising to take care of it, and me ending up with most of the work and all of the expense. We had many such animals over the years, and many interesting stories about these American pedigrees, the mongrel mixes so reflective of the American culture. I considered them to be of a far superior breed.

Jasper was the aging alpha dog, constantly challenged by the rambunctious young Tulip. I carried my machete to whack at vines and wave in front of me when I got into the woods to cut through the spider webs that were so numerous this time of year. We were winding down along the path when I first spotted him. The dogs had taken off on a run after some scent. I looked up way ahead through the woods and saw a man lumbering along the winding path toward me. He was tall, lean and black. He wore a long, colorful dashiki over loose white trousers. His stride was long and rhythmic, and he was waving a long, gleaming machete that made mine look small and inadequate. As he wound his way towards me, he suddenly caught my eye. His face lit up and his eyes sparkled, his stride unchanged.

It would be a serious understatement to say this was a shock to me. I live way out in the country and never have trespassers except for the occasional stray hunter. There are few people of color in the entire county, and certainly none with such strange dress and bearing. When he saw me, he walked on towards me without the slightest hesitation, as though he expected to see me or was about to greet someone he knew. I heard the dogs racing through the woods towards us and was comforted, fully expecting that they would give this stranger the hostile greeting any unknown creature received when venturing into their territory. To my amazement, they simply wagged their tails and ran up to him, seeking his attention as though he were an old friend.

By this time, he was close to me, within twenty feet or so. I could see that he was indeed a tall man, well over six feet. He had high cheek bones and was wearing leather sandals. I spoke first. "Hello there. Are you lost? Can I help you?" I said rather coldly, trying my best to display my distain for trespassers while maintaining a proper etiquette.

He stopped a few feet in front of me. "Yes sir. I am indeed lost as you say, but I doubt that you can help me."

He had a foreign accent, the clear diction and delivery of an African. He squatted on his haunches, placed his machete on the ground in front of him and began petting the still excited dogs. They calmed immediately with his gentle touch.

"My name is Jo-seph," he said, "and I am far from home, yet it is right here."

Oh great, I thought, so now I have a foreigner on my property who speaks in riddles. I began searching my brain for anything I may have learned from local news and gossip sources recently that would help explain this odd visitor. He was too old, it seemed to me, to be one of those high school exchange students. I guessed his age to be somewhere in the late twenties to early thirties. The lack of any local strategic importance made me discard the notion that he may be a terrorist. But what was he doing here? He certainly didn't walk from Africa.

I suddenly felt awkward standing over him, still firmly gripping my puny machete. I am short, about five feet seven, and standing there I was just barely above him as he comfortably rested on his haunches. He seemed in excellent shape. If it came to a physical confrontation here in the woods he could no doubt tear me from limb to limb. There happened to be a tree stump right there at the side of the trail, where I had cut away a fallen hickory the year before. I sat down on it and placed my machete across my knees. I admired his ability to squat so comfortably, without the need of anything to sit upon. Even if I had not had that knee surgery many years ago, I doubt I could squat like that.

"I have come from far away, yet very close. Everything around me is so strange yet so familiar. You see I am not from your world at all. Times like this I think I should never have volunteered to be part of the noble scientific venture that has captured me in its vortex."

He must be mentally ill. Perhaps he walked away from some treatment facility, but the nearest psychiatric hospital was in the city, over sixty miles away. "Did you walk here from the town?" I asked, assuming my therapist demeanor.

"The town? No, no," he said and began to laugh in an easy and relaxed fashion. "I've come from many towns, in various realms and realities. You see, I am trying to find my way back to the point in time when things went wrong. My trouble is that I have been through so many time zones and warps that I am befuddled."

That makes two of us, I thought. My cell phone was back at the house. If I could just get to it I could call the authorities and get the poor man back to a safe place. He obviously needed to be in a secure environment, where his delusional thinking could be treated. I had to handle this delicately, given the fact that he was armed and perhaps dangerous. My eyes fixed on the long, sharp blade of his machete. He noticed this.

"I mean you no harm," he said. "I know this must sound very strange to you. You see I am a traveler from a parallel universe. I volunteered to participate in a scientific experiment with a noble purpose. I entered a hole in space and now I am lost. I know this is hard to believe, but I am telling you the truth. I am not insane, though I know I seem so to you. We are closely related in some way that confounds our understanding. That must be why I got here at this point in time and space. There is some reason, if I can only figure it out. The link between us is strong, distant and close at the same time."

"Perhaps I can help you," I said. "Let's walk up to the house. I will get you a cool drink and we can talk about it."

"Thank you for your kind offer," he said with sincerity. "But I will leave you now."

He rose, grabbed his machete and raised it high above his head, all in one motion. What happened then was so incredible and unbelievable that I cannot even believe it now as I retell it. He sliced the blade down across the space in front of him. It was the most astonishing thing. He sliced through the visual field as though it were a movie screen, as though everything I was seeing and accepted as reality was just a projection.

It ripped like cloth. Then he raised his long arm again. The tip of the machete, high above me, sparkled as it caught a ray of sun. The look on his face was serene. Again, he sliced the air, ripping my world. The two cuts crossed and I could see through the hole into a whirling nothingness. All around the hole my world was just the same, three-dimensional and normal. There was forest and fauna and the gentle rustling of the autumn leaves. In the middle was this huge hole ripped to expose another dimension. It was like something I once saw in a cartoon.

The dogs whimpered and cowered in the brush. I lost my balance and fell backwards off the log, landing in a mattress of undergrowth and crisp leaves. I looked up at the hole. Jo-seph stood facing it, his back to me. He was fully erect and calm, staring into the pulsating, alluring world behind the screen. It looked and smelled like nothing I have ever experienced. Then he coiled his long body like a cat and leapt into that void. The hole quickly healed and the world was back to normal. I staggered to my feet and stared at the place the hole had been in disbelief. I slowly, fearfully, stretched out my arm to touch the surface where the hole had been. I felt nothing but air, no resistance whatever, but the familiar annoyance of a spider web sticking to my hand.

My heart was racing, my mind a blur. I stumbled back the path to the house. It is a steep climb. I made it up to the meadow and turned to face the sky. The autumn sun shown on the valley. The air was sharp and fresh. All seemed so normal. I could not catch my breath. I fell on my back and could not move. I suspected I was having a stroke as the result of a psychotic episode. Then all went black.

I have no idea how long I was unconscious. I felt a sensation on my face that alerted my brain. I realized I was alive. The dogs were licking my face. I had to inventory my senses. First priority, after calming the insistent and needy dogs, was to calm my heart. Difficult as it was, I managed to take several deep breaths, in through the nose, held for the count of three, and out through the mouth. It worked enough for me to somehow sit up, then get to my feet and finish the journey home. All the way I tried to make sense of it all.

What could have brought on this hallucination, the death of my wife, my loneliness? While I missed my wife and her death was a shock, I had been adjusting. I enjoyed my solitude. I did not feel lonely and I had no history of mental illness. I thought of all the clients I had in therapy over the years who had hallucinations. Invariably there was a family history, a personal history, a triggering trauma. My family had no exceptional history of mental illness that I was aware of, certainly nothing so close on the family tree of such intensity. There was my father's brother who was rather strange. As kids, I and my sibs called him weird Uncle Frank. He spent a lot of time chasing demons.

Now my own have come back to life, the dark corners of my childhood, the thing under the bed.

My mind was racing and shifting gears much too rapidly. I had to center myself and control my breathing. I spent the next few days in periods of meditation and fending off anxiety attacks. I stopped answering email and the phone. I somehow went about daily routines such as feeding the animals and brushing my teeth, yet ignored others. My hygiene and appetite suffered. Sleep was a struggle, restless nights and irregular periods of deep slumber, often ending with a shocking awakening, overcome by the feeling that someone was in the house. I was losing my mind. I knew I should get help, but could not bring myself to do so. I always encouraged clients to talk things out. I knew it was what I should do, but with whom?

One day I found myself curled up under the covers of my bed, drifting in and out of frightful sleep, when a knock came to the door. I hadn't even heard the car driving down the lane. I tried to ignore the knocking, but it just got more persistent. I got out of bed and realized I was still in my pajamas. The clock on my dresser said it was 7 pm but did not tell me the day, month, or year. I had lost all track of time.

I put on my bathrobe and peeked out the window. A furious wind was driving a wet snow. I couldn't see who was at the door, but I recognized the car in the parking area. It was my friend, Roger. I went to the door and opened it. He took one look at me and his jaw dropped. His eyes glazed over like ice on the pond. I recognized that look on his face. It was the same one he had when his wife left him several years ago. It lasted for weeks. We stood there looking at each other in appraisal for what seemed like forever. "You look like shit," he said, nudging his way in the door.

He had been trying to reach me for days he said. When I missed the Arts Council meeting he started getting worried. I was in charge of the upcoming spring arts festival and was supposed to give an update at the meeting. He got no response from emails or phone messages. Suddenly the franticly flickering answering machine caught my eye across the room. When was the last time I punched its buttons? He was so worried about me that he decided to drive out after work to see if I was all right.

My first instinct was to tell him I was sick and contagious, but getting better and in need of no help, and send him away. I did not want to see, much less talk, to anyone. But the weather was miserable and the drive back long. He needed so much help getting that look off his face when his marriage ended. Now he got it again by looking at me. I could not remember when I last looked in a mirror. I must look a wreck to him as I would to anyone else. A stranger would likely view me as deranged and dangerous. I invited him in, babbling reassurances and stumbling to the kitchen to play host. Coffee or tea? What about me? We settled into reasonable repartee. The discourse helped my mind to focus through the fog. The sudden responsibility to participate in conversation was sobering. I apologized profusely for missing the meeting and told him I was sick, but getting better, I think. I stopped short of telling him about Joseph. We sat, drank bitter coffee, and enjoyed each other's company.

When he left, I began getting my life back in order. I took a shower and cleaned up the house some. I went through my phone messages and emails. I have a Luddite aversion to new tech. I don't text or twitter. I have to draw a line somewhere. Reconnecting with the world kept me busy as I went about the tasks involved in getting the homestead prepared for winter. Somehow, I got through the holidays.

The winter was dark and wicked, with record snows and bitter winds. I had no problem keeping busy during the day, but the nights were frightful. Day by day I was encouraged by the lack of any reoccurrence of hallucinations. I convinced myself that it was an isolated incident, probably caused by something I ate, and unlikely to reoccur. Telling myself this helped me sleep. Then in early spring I was out in the garden, preparing beds for planting. I had my foot on a pitchfork I was using to test the soil. I heard something sounding like static from a radio caught between stations. It came and went, and was accompanied by a flickering like a butterfly in my peripheral vision. I raised my head to look.

I saw an image coming and going with the static, trying to come into focus. I could not make it out at first. I froze and stared. When the static increased all other sounds, the birds, the dogs, the wind stopped. My normal auditory world was gone. I could not believe what I saw. The image was a little man in a green suit looking just like a cartoon leprechaun on a Saint Patrick's Day card. He was barely over five feet tall and had a round little belly. He had a straggly gray beard and was holding a shillelagh. The static stopped and the image stabilized. The little man stared and me and said, "Top of the morning to ya!" I stumbled back over a bucket and fell on my butt. Between us was the pitch fork, stuck in the ground. I felt a need to seize it.

Instead I pushed myself back on my feet and fled to the house.

I ran in, locked the door and went to the study window, where I could see the apparition partially obscured by the boughs of the white pine. He was standing there, about fifteen yards away, seemingly fidgeting with his pockets and the folds of his tight fitting little suit. I shuddered and shook and looked around me in all directions, fearing I would see another strange being. Then I saw a vehicle driving down my lane towards the house. As it got closer I realized it was Roger's pick-up truck, with Roger at the wheel and someone next to him in the passenger's seat. It was Teresa Baxter, a dear friend and widow who had taken a particular interest in my welfare since my wife's death.

The truck slowed to a stop next to the garden. Roger lowered his window, poked out his head and started talking to the apparition. The little man responded, taking a few steps towards the vehicle and looking at Roger. Teresa leaned over and looked at the man. I could see their lips moving but could not hear their words. The look of shock was on all three faces. Shock bolted through me, then the soothing sensation of mental and physical relief. I was not hallucinating.

That was the good news. The truth was even stranger than that.

I turned from the window to run to the door and caught my reflection in the floor length mirror on the wall. I locked onto my eyes. I saw the face of a mad man. I stumbled on the way out the door and up the lane. When I got to the truck the little man was mumbling something in what sounded like a thick Irish brogue, totally unintelligible. He was fumbling through the many pockets of his funny green suit. He looked at me and said, "I'll just be a moment now, where in #%& did I put it?"

He was full of energy and jittery motion. Roger and Teresa looked at me in wonder. I told them I had no idea where he came from, and that I thought I was hallucinating. The man looked back and me and said, "Ah now, you remember me lad. I'm Joseph. We met down in the woods last fall, when the sun was bright and the air was full of wonder."

He pulled a pocket knife from his vest and opened the blade. "I'm sorry if I have inconvenienced you in any way. I know this is difficult for you to understand. It is confusing to me as well, but I must be off now." He turned and raised his arm above his head. I froze, audibly sucking in air, fully expecting my world

to rip apart again. He slashed the air with his knife.
Nothing happened. He slashed again and again,
swinging his arm, making a huge X in the air over and
over. The knife seemed much longer than it had been
when he pulled it from his pocket. It had gone from a
tiny little blade of about two inches, to a shining saber
of eleven inches or more. When he raised it high, the
sun caught the blade and struck my eyes, blinding me
briefly. Using my hand as a visor I could see that still
nothing had happened.

I heard a startled cry. It was coming from
Teresa. I turned and saw she was reaching down into
her purse. I realized she was searching for her cell
phone. Roger's face turned cold. He shifted the truck
into gear and tore off down the lane. He turned hard
at the house and the truck came to an abrupt stop. I
heard Teresa again, this time an anguished howl as she
lurched forward and dumped the contents of her purse.

I headed for them as quickly as I could. I heard
a strange screech from the little man behind me. I
turned. He had dropped the knife and was holding his
hands in the air. He walked out of the garden and
started down the lane. "I'm so sorry to disturb you,"
he shouted in a high voice filled with the flavor of
Ireland. "I mean ya no harm. I can explain. Look, I've
put down the knife. I have no weapon, and I'd be

foolish now to take on two big strong men as I'm seeing before me. My dear mother didn't raise a fool, God rest her soul." At this he took off his hat and held it to his heart. "Please, I am a peaceful man. Let me explain." Then the dogs appeared from the woods and ran happily towards the little man, panting and wagging their tails.

We gathered at the front of the house. The little man babbled on. He was amazingly spry, arriving between Roger and me while Teresa was still in the truck fumbling for her cell phone. He probed the distance of our personal space, advancing then retreating. He said he was a lost visitor from another dimension. He somehow got stuck here with us when something went wrong with the noble experiment of Doctor Nomo to probe the layers of existence present in any one space at any one time. "I really don't understand it myself," he said. "I'm not a scientist myself. I just volunteered because I needed the money and it sounded like quite an adventure. I'm just finding my way back and then I will quit this job and go back to my normal life. I've had enough adventure for several lifetimes. I just want to go home." He looked us straight in the eye pleadingly. He seemed so sincere.

He had dropped his shillelagh and outer clothing—hat, coat, vest and shirt—along the way down the lane. He said he was trying to show us that he had no weapons. He had his thumbs tucked under the broad suspenders strapped over his long-johns and holding up his trousers. He slid his thumbs up and down behind the straps, tugging in such a fashion that I feared he was about to slide them off and drop his drawers.

Teresa was with us now, holding her cell phone, ready to call for help and looking just as befuddled as the Roger and I. Just then a low thunderhead rolled in from the southeast. Dark clouds seldom come from that direction, but when they do they are usually quick and violent. Flashes of lightening pulsated through the sky and suddenly in my head as well. My vision went black and my mind washed clean for a nanosecond. It happened once and then a second time, then a third, all within about two minutes, timed to the flashes of distant lightning. I was having mini-blackouts. Then I heard Theresa: "Oh shit! What was that? Why did everything go blank?"

All the world was wobbly. I could tell from their faces that both Roger and Teresa were having the seizures also. "Damn it!" said the little man "I hate it when that happens. Why can't they get that straight?"

"Who?" asked Roger.

258

"Why the #%@# scientist of course," answered the little man.

"What's happening here? Do you know this guy?" Roger asked me. I had to sit down. I had to get inside. I was covered with mud from my fall in the garden. The dogs were so excited they would not settle down, going from one of us to another, licking and demanding attention. Their tails wagged frantically. It was about to rain. I turned to the house. Somehow, we all got in the house and to the kitchen, leaving the dogs behind. Through the window, I saw the dogs having a tug-of-war with the little man's coat. Then a bolt of lightning struck the pond. The dogs ran for the barn and the sky dropped a deluge of rain. The little man pulled up a chair and sat at the table, making himself comfortable. Teresa and Roger stood, shuffling their feet and looking stunned. I went into auto-drive, putting the kettle on the stove and getting out the tea, as though this were a common social gathering.

"Yes, yes, a spot of tea would be nice my lad," said the little man. "And would it be possible to have a nip of whisky as well, just enough to take the chill off?" he added with a wink and a twinkle in his eye. I got out a bottle of Jameson I had left over from a St. Patty's party a few years ago. I got some glasses from the cupboard and poured out a round. I was helpless to reply in any meaningful way to such absurd speech. He was more caricature than person. I still wondered if he were an illusion. I reached out my arm. I had to find out. He flinched slightly when I touched his shoulder. Actually, it was more like an electrical charge that passed between us, startling us both.

"What, how, you say you are the same being I met last fall?" I stammered. "How could that be? What are you?"

He grabbed the bottle, topped off his glass and slugged it down before answering. "They don't seem to have the ethnic synchronization working either. They come close sometimes, but it just is never quite right, and they seem to have no feeling for what these sudden and bizarre transformations are doing to me."

"Who?" asked Teresa, trying to get a handle on the situation.

"The frigging scientist," the little man exploded. "I just told ya. They don't know what they're doing; fooling around with parallel universes and anti-matter as though there was no danger at all. I hope I live through this, and long enough to write a book exposing the arrogance and hubris of the over-educated idgets and their infernal experiments."

Roger stepped between Teresa and the man in such a protective way that I wondered if my two friends were sleeping together. What a strange thought to have at such a time. Perhaps my mental status was even worse than I believed. Just then the kettle started to whistle. I turned to the stove and, as I was moving it from the hot burner I heard a chair slide across the floor. I turned back and saw the man rise to his feet. He stared intensely out the window. Roger was mumbling something about telling this to the authorities. The rain had stopped, the storm had passed as suddenly as it had come, and there was a rainbow arching the sky.

"That's it!" the little man shouted.

He darted to the door, almost knocking over Roger and Teresa. We quickly followed him and watched as he strolled confidently up the lane and slowly vanished. He just vanished. We looked at each other. Roger was the first to speak, "Hooolllllly shit! What the hell just happened?" His words were long and drawn out and just hung there in the air.

Now, one year later, we are still trying to answer that question. New bonds have formed between us. Teresa and I are occasional lovers and I think she is sleeping with Roger as well, which is fine with me and apparently fine with my two friends. Teresa is a great girl. I don't mind sharing. We got together on the anniversary of the event, March 17th. We recreated each step, word, and movement as best we could, up to when he disappeared, then the bewilderment that follows us still. Our search of the area immediately after the incident turned up no evidence of the man at all. The clothes he shed and the knife he discarded were nowhere to be found.

After the incident, Teresa and Roger grilled me relentlessly about my first encounter with Joseph that fall day in the woods, obviously annoyed that I did not tell them about it at the time. I apologized, but I got them to admit that they would not have believed me, nor would anyone believe the three of us about our Saint Patrick's Day leprechaun. We discussed this late into the night.

Teresa was insistent at first that we had to report this to the authorities, some authority, somehow. We played out various possibilities. Each ended with us the subjects of ridicule. In the end, we agreed that we would tell no one, at least until we all had more of a chance to think about it. I am confident that sooner or later word will get out. Teresa may tell a friend in her quilting group. Roger may tell the therapist he has been seeing since his divorce. I may even tell someone myself, though I have no idea who it would be. I feel a tugging to tell someone outside of our circle for some reason, which is probably why I am writing this down now, in hopes of leaving a record for someone to find.

In the past year, we have each searched the internet for information on parallel universes, trying to sort out the truth from the garbage. We have also searched our souls looking for personal answers. Teresa and Roger have become more religious. They have joined a Unitarian church, engaging in endless discussions about the meaning of life. They want me to join, but I have resisted, viewing it as a prime vehicle for leaks. I'm not ready for public disclosure.

On the anniversary, we talked late into the night. We took out the bottle of whiskey which had been untouched since the incident. We poured three glasses and toasted Joseph, wishing him well wherever he is.

Bird Feeding

"Jays are more gang than flock" said Jake, the crow.

He is a bird of few words. We'd been discussing the blue jays that have been visiting and cleaning out the suet feeders lately, much to the dismay of both of us.

It was a cool and crisp spring morning. The sky was clearing after a substantial rain. I took a deep breath, trying to suck in as much of it as I could. The air was full of the sounds of cardinals, chickadees, tanagers and wrens, the sweet smell of blossoms, wet and beckoning. Gone was the bell-like trill of the dark-eyed juncos, headed north to breed.

"Good riddance," said Jake.

The jays have two distinct advantages over Jake at the suet feeder. One is that they can eat underneath without scaring away the wood peckers and song birds feasting on the suet cakes above, dropping chunks and scraps aplenty below. When Jake tries this, he scares them all away.

"Maybe it's your personality," I suggested.

"Caw!" said Jake.

Jake is big and boisterous and seemingly oblivious to how he is perceived by others. He is the kind of guy you would try to avoid at a party, and one I wish to keep off my bird feeders. But I like him. I try to help him out from time to time with some suggestions and insights from a human perspective.

"Trouble with you f&#@*%g humans is you think you know everything. If ya ain't got wings, ya ain't got no idea what it's like."

I resisted trying to explain how two negatives make a positive. Much as I have tried, there are some things that I just can't get through to that bird.

The second advantage the jays have is that, unlike Jake, they can feed directly on the suet cakes, scaring away all but the bigger wood peckers and flickers that hold their place even when the jays do their dive-bombing maneuvers. Pickings below were slim these days for Jake. He tried perching on the suet cakes, but that was futile. He is just too big and lacks the marvelous ability of woodpeckers to cling on a vertical surface. Jake was beside himself. He finally was rid of the juncos and now he had this to contend with.

For me the problem is one of economics. I have been going through suet cakes, at a buck each, like flap-jacks at a Kiwanis breakfast. I just can't go on like this. So, when it comes to Jays at the suet, Jake and I can relate. Jake is most articulate when he is complaining about something. This is another keen observation of mine he does not care to hear.

Over the years, I have tried to adapt the feeders to attract only the birds I want, warding off the obnoxious heavy eaters—varmints such as squirrels and raccoons and certainly birds like Jake. It is an endless pursuit. Just when you think you get one problem solved it comes back again, or another rises to replace the first.

Squirrels are tough little suckers. Jake is right about that. They climb and jump and descend from above. They plot against us at night and launch covert operations and surgical strikes. By almost every measure, they are smarter than we are.

I tried greasing the pole on the feeder that sticks in the ground and setting up all kinds of obstacles. I bought a squirrel-proof feeder to hang from a tree. I wrapped chicken wire around the pole feeder. It looked like the creation of a mad orthodontist. But it worked. Not only did it keep out the squirrels, it kept out all the birds.

I grew the hottest of the hot peppers, dried them and grated them into a fine powder. I mixed it in with the bird seed. I had read that this works. Birds digest the powder without distress, but not so squirrels. I watched from the house as, one by one the squirrels climbed up the pole to the feeder, got a snout full of pepper, and ran away rubbing at eyes and mouth. I was delighted. I thought that would be the end of the problem. Then one squirrel climbed the pole and started eating. He took his first bite, shook his head and wiped his nose, and went right back to feeding. Having a 99.9% deterrent rate is not good enough for squirrels. Just one is enough to quickly empty a feeder.

The squirrel who ate through my hot pepper defense is Pedro. He comes from a long line of Mexican squirrels that migrated north, illegally I suspect. I hear he likes tequila.

So, I purchased a baffle, a slick metal cylinder that goes around the pole. So far it is working. If it fails, I am thinking of digging moats around our feeders and filling in with either alligators or nuclear waste. Which do you think would work best?

To keep the deer and rabbits out of the vegetable garden, I'm thinking of installing two, parallel, 12-foot-high chain-link fences around the perimeter, with vicious canines patrolling the space between. Maybe I could capture some coyotes for the job. But the garden is another story.

"You're getting slow, Jake. You've been eating too much of that field corn. Don't you know they treat it with Atrazine?"

I'm always trying to be helpful. I try to explain that studies show small amounts of Atrazine can turn otherwise healthy male frogs into hermaphrodites.

"Hermafra-whatee?" asks Jake.

I explain. He is suddenly concerned. He looks down between his legs and up at me again.

"Ya mean that could happen to me?"

I tell him that it won't change him but could affect his offspring. I don't know if this could happen. I figure Jake won't do the research. I got his attention. It is for his own good to be more concerned about what he eats.

"Too late to worry about that."

Jake, relieved of the worry, goes back to hunting suet scraps.

"Frogs is good though," he says, "specially when they's young."

Then he gets angry at me again.

"Let me see if I got this straight. You feed the woodpeckers and what do they do? They drill holes in your house. I help clean up your mess by getting rid of your road-kills, but you don't feed me. Hey, I wouldn't have to eat so much field corn if ya just would put out more sunflower seed!"

I'm staring up at the sky when he says this, and suddenly it dawns on me.

"So you're the one that's been raiding the sunflower feeders, and I thought it was squirrels!"

I turn to look at him and he is taking flight, turning, unfurling his powerful wings, springing off his strong legs. I hear him laughing as he quickly flies out of site over the tall pines.

"Caw, caw, caw, caw"

ACKNOWLEDGMENTS

Many thanks to my wife, Marty, who edited this book and continues to provide me with laughter, love and various other forms of support. In spite of all the evidence to the contrary, it is possible for a marriage to survive such a collaboration.

Many thanks to Marty's brother-in-law, Bob Lough, who's magical tech skills produced the cover art. He is a wizard, a friend and occasional travel companion.

Many thanks to John Grisham, Sue Grafton, Mark McLane, David McCullough, and so many other popular authors who had nothing directly to do with this book except to inspire me to write.

Many thanks to my brothers and sisters and children for providing me with a lifetime of stories and love. I hope they are not offended by what I wrote, though they are likely to have memories of the events that differ in some respects from my accounts. Most likely they will remind me of so many other stories I have left out.

Last but far from least, thanks to Helen Herrmann and Charles Cooney (AKA: Mom and Dad). Their love is what brought us into the world and kept us together. Without them this book would never have happened.